To Zeno

May your adventuresome
spirit continue to fill
your life.
    all the Best

        Stg

The Road Taken paints a compelling picture of bicycle travel by recent college graduates, and it brought back many happy memories of my own cross-country bicycle trip. Touring by bicycle is a great way to experience a country, and this book highlights the joys and challenges that a small group of friends experienced during the early years of riding a bicycle across the U.S. The story is further enhanced by interweaving stories among the individual cyclists and the connections with historical events along the route, and by its recognition of the role that bicycling can play in our modern society as a means to promote environmental and human health.

RICHARD WEISMAN

Career Civil Servant
Bicycle Enthusiast

This short book is so much more than the sum of its parts. Granted, the mostly understated accounts of daily struggles, seemingly insuperable obstacles, and narrow escapes from life-threatening disasters over the course of more than 3,000 miles make for compelling reading and kept me glued to the page from start to finish.

Persistence is surely the dominant theme. How could soon-to-be college grads, sensible science and math majors all, find it in themselves and each other to just keep turning the pedals day after day after long day for a month and more?

In retrospect, though, I was even more grateful for the book's underlying themes and values: youth, camaraderie, determination, the glories (and harshness) of nature, the kindness of strangers for just a few.

Looking back, I love especially the last word of the title, "Odyssey." Unfortunately, Homer never had a chance to ride a bike, but if he had I am convinced he would have recognized and applauded the high spirit of adventure drawn from universal values on which The Road Taken is based.

PHILIP COVINGTON
US Foreign Service Officer, Retired

In 1972 five Duke seniors celebrated their graduation and the beginning of a new life by riding their bicycles across America. This is a delightful account of serendipity, the generosity of strangers, and perseverance as they pedaled west against stronger winds and tougher terrain than they imagined. You will enjoy reading about their odyssey as much as they enjoyed the ride.

CHAZ MILLER
Long-time bicycle rider and enthusiast

An interesting, well-written account of recent college grads who bicycled cross-country in 1972, during relatively simpler times. Despite many challenges, their determination helped them meet this huge physical accomplishment. They learned a lot about the generosity of diverse people across the country and experienced the beauty of rural America from a bicycle seat. They slept in jails, primitive campsites (with no tent!), and while riding endured heat, humidity, headwinds, hills, and getting separated from each other. This easy-to-read, adventurous but down to earth story includes historic text boxes and trip photos. The book offers good tips for long-distance bike touring. Readers will learn how their travels and experiences impacted their lives, families and future careers.

DARRYL CARON
Founder/Publisher, Adirondack Sports Magazine,
Who Also Bicycled Cross-Country In 1987

THE
ROAD
TAKEN

The Remarkable Story of a Transcontinental Bicycle Odyssey

BRYAN SIMMONS, STIG REGLI, AND BILL JACKSON

EDMONDS PRESS
Watertown, MN

EDMONDS PRESS
an imprint of Excegent Communication

Watertown, Minnesota, USA

Library of Congress Control Number: 2021932963

Primary printing in the United States, POD in other locations.
Published by Edmonds Press, an imprint of Excegent
Communication, LLC.
www.edmondspress.com

*The Road Taken: The Remarkable Story of a
Transcontinental Bicycle Odyssey*
First Edition
Bryan Simmons, Stig Regli, and Bill Jackson

Cover Design, Map, and Layout by Najdan Mancic
Copyedit by Hazel Walshaw
Stephen W. Jones, General Editor
The following are used by permission:
    "They are on their way to the pacific" photo: Yadkin Ripple
    Quote from Times-Journal
    Cannon Beach brochure cover
    Golden West Cafe menu

ISBN: 978-1-940105-12-3 Paperback
ISBN: 978-1-940105-13-0 Hardcover
ISBN: 978-1-940105-15-4 Kindle
ISBN: 978-1-940105-14-7 Ebook

TRV026100 TRAVEL / Special Interest / Bicycling
SPO011000 SPORTS & RECREATION / Cycling
BIO026000 BIOGRAPHY & AUTOBIOGRAPHY / Personal Memoirs

I dedicate this book to my mother, who encouraged me to take the bicycle trip, paid for it, accepted my weekly "collect" phone calls, and saved every single postcard from the trip that I sent her.

BRYAN

To my wife Melanie and daughters Kirsten and Jocelyn.

STIG

TABLE OF CONTENTS

Note for the reader: most of the book is a first-person narrative by two separate authors, Bryan Simmons and, starting with Chapter Five "A New Start For Stig," Stig Regli. At that point they alternate as authors with each chapter.

ACKNOWLEDGEMENTS

I want to thank my wife Barbara, my good friend Paul Matthews, and John Jones, for their encouragement to expand my preliminary draft into a book.

BRYAN

I am forever grateful to my mother who instilled a sense of wonder and adventure in life. I am grateful to the many people that helped me during this trip. I am grateful to Aarne Vesilind, Donald Wright, and Dennis Warner who mentored me at Duke before and after my bicycling travels to elucidate a career path forward.

STIG

We are also grateful to Stephen, Jennie, and John Jones for their editing and good work in bringing the manuscript to publication.

THE AUTHORS

FOREWORD

BY MICHAEL COX

Former Environmental Protection Agency Climate Change Advisor and local climate activist

In 1972, five students from Duke University embarked on an odyssey. Four of them completed a bicycle journey across the United States and the other biker completed a very impressive 1000-mile trip. Their journey was powered by a desire for adventure, an interest to connect with people, and a need to test their physical abilities. They actually referred to the trip as an "Odyssey" for several reasons (see if you can find the references to Homer's *The Odyssey* in the book).

Their trip reminds me of my own bike trip after I graduated from college in 1981. I took a 2-month bike trip through Washington, Oregon, Idaho, and British Columbia with two friends. Many of the stories from the book resonated with me and brought a smile to my face and, at times, a grimace at the painful reminder of some of the harder times. Their 100 mile per day average for an entire month, with all the challenges they encountered, is particularly impressive. I am sure others have done similar adventures and the book will bring back the mostly fond memories of their own journeys.

In 1972, the issue of climate change was not front-page news, but scientists were starting to recognize its importance. In the years following the bicycle odyssey across America, this issue certainly has driven the life of both author Stig Regli and myself. Driven by a combination of factors including the need for exercise, the desire to avoid contributing to pollution from cars, and as a small part of our own roles in reducing greenhouse gas emissions, both Stig and I rode our bikes to work for over 25 years.

We find ourselves now in a climate crisis of our own making, to which we must respond. The urgent need to substantially reduce our greenhouse gas emissions and make our communities more resilient against climate change requires that we take significant action now. Waiting puts our communities, economies, and our children's futures in peril.

A 2018 report from the Intergovernmental Panel on Climate Change[1] stated that to keep global temperatures below a 1.5°C increase compared to pre-industrial levels will require net zero global carbon emis-

---

[1]   IPCC, 2018: Summary for Policymakers. In: Global warming of 1.5°C. An IPCC Special Report on the impacts of global warming of 1.5°C above pre-industrial levels and related global greenhouse gas emission pathways, in the context of strengthening the global response to the threat of climate change, sustainable development, and efforts to eradicate poverty. https://www.ipcc.ch/sr15/

sions by approximately 2050. This conclusion is also supported by the 4th National Climate Assessment.[2]

Nationally, the U.S. transportation sector contributes almost 30 percent of our country's total greenhouse gas emissions. Locally, the contribution can be much higher. For example, in Washington State, where I live, the transportation sector contributes over 45 percent of the greenhouse gas emissions in the State.

In order to meet our national and state goals for reducing greenhouse gases we need to transform our transportation systems. Experience in other communities and countries shows that safe, convenient, and attractive networks of cycling and walking pathways for all ages and abilities — well-linked from residential areas to employment, school, and shopping — are required to significantly increase participation in biking and walking. Such networks *must* include separated or protected bike lanes. While some communities are making progress, others are lagging behind in creating such networks.

An example of a successful project is the Burke-Gilman Trail in the Seattle area. It is a 27-mile off-road multi-use trail that connects communities throughout the region to downtown Seattle. The trail has become a major transportation corridor that serves thousands

---

[2]   Fourth National Climate Assessment. Volume 11: Impacts, Risks, and Adaptation in the United States. 2018. https://nca2018.globalchange.gov/

of commuter and recreational cyclists each day. The Burke-Gilman Trail demonstrates that when the proper facilities are provided, many people will choose healthy, pollution-free, non-motorized modes of travel.

In addition, in order to make this necessary transition, it will be important to promote mixed-use development and multi-family housing in core areas in order to enable greater use of non-motorized transportation options and prioritize new transit-oriented development.

Because of COVID-19, many people have decided that they are not comfortable taking public transportation anytime soon. One silver lining in this trend is a 60% surge in national bike sales, including a large increase in electric bikes, since March 2020.

But, in order for people to actually use bikes as their primary or secondary mode of transportation, there must be a safe network of routes for people to utilize. The main reason people do not use their bikes as a primary or secondary mode of transportation is that they do not feel safe.

Of course, getting people out of their cars and onto their bikes will reduce our greenhouse gas emissions. However, it will also provide health benefits to the riders, reduce undesirable health impacts to people from air pollution caused by cars and trucks, and provide jobs for people at bike shops and for the outdoor recreational business.

We also have an obligation to our children, grandchildren, nieces, nephews, and neighbors to leave this place we call home a better place than what we inherited. That means we need to not only advocate for change, but we must also model beneficial behaviors that our children will see and emulate.

We cannot all complete a cross-country bike adventure to show our support for addressing climate change. We can, however, take advantage of the surge of interest in biking to advocate nationally, and in our own communities, to create the biking and walking networks needed to get people out of their cars and onto their bikes.

I encourage you to read this excellent travel adventure of five intrepid Duke students to provide you with encouragement to start riding your bike to both help address climate change, and for your own wellbeing.

INTRODUCTION

I was one of five students at Duke University in Durham, NC, wanting upon graduation, in May 1972, to do something physically memorable, and perhaps transformative for the rest of our lives. We all recognized that once we were on a career path, the opportunities for alternative adventures and discoveries could shrink drastically, and before we knew it, we might be old men not capable of such pursuits. Furthermore, the prospect of doing something together and having each other's support was particularly appealing. Our aspirations for travel in 1972 may have been unconsciously reinforced by major events in the US: President Nixon ordering the development of the space shuttle program (January 5); *Mariner 9* sending its first pictures from Mars (February 4); and the Pioneer 10 spacecraft being launched from Cape Kennedy, the first man-made satellite to leave the solar system (March 2). However, we were more interested in exploring the vast unknowns of our own country rather than that of the universe.

Four of us (Bill Jackson, Hal Hemme, Vaughn Lamb and me, Bryan Simmons) were close friends living in the same dormitory. We had toyed with hiking the Appalachian Trail, which can take a year to cover a significant distance, but we decided to do a cross-county bike trip due to Vaughn's commitment to start a job at Duke' Marine Lab on June 19th. We envisioned that biking cross-country would offer broad opportunities, socially and geographically, to discover much of our country that we knew little about. Little did we know at that time that we would be confronted with so many unexpected events and challenges. These included overwhelming winds, torrential rains, extreme heat, life threatening gunshots from strangers, sleeping in jails, bicycle accidents, and the separation of our group that changed the dynamics of the whole adventure. Also, serendipitous meetings with remarkable people at critical junctures uplifted us in times of greatest need.

Stig Regli, who did not know us initially, had been contemplating a possible around the world bicycle trip in search of meaning for his life. He had not found any willing partners and did not have the courage to do this alone. When he learned about our plans for doing a cross-county trip he became interested in joining us. Stig had to be back in Durham during the last week in June for a friend's wedding, so the timing fit well with our plans.

I had a mediocre history of athletic accomplishments up until the bike trip. I walked 25 miles at age 12 in response to President Kennedy's clarion call for increased physical fitness. After the walk, my back went into painful spasms that confined me to bed for almost a week. I was an average runner on my high school cross-country running team. Together with Bill and Hal, I jogged frequently at Duke University covering two miles back and forth between Duke's two campuses sometimes several times per week. Hal came in 21st in the one-mile inter-campus Cake Run contest; the cheerleaders gave the first 20 finishers a cake (no piece of cake for Hal). Bill, Hal, and I were very active on the Windsor dormitory intramural sports team, and our dorm won the school intramural championship three years in a row, retiring the trophy. Dormitories at Duke acted as local fraternities at the time and competed in intramural sports against all other dormitories, including the dormitories of national fraternities. None of us were avid bikers.

Stig had a bicycle that he sometimes used to commute to his classes on campus from where he lived off campus. He also played intramural tennis and basketball and played golf with some members of Duke's golf team. In an indication of what was to come, Stig had a penchant for physical extremes. He once played 144 holes of golf in one day in Denmark with four of his close friends. During his junior year at Duke, Stig had a bet with one of Duke's fabled beer drinkers that Stig could walk or run more miles than John could drink beers, each in one day. Stig covered 68 miles in 16 hours but the bet was annulled when John threatened to induce self-vomiting to increase his beer drinking capacity.

All five cyclists were good students at Duke. Bill had a double major in mathematics and economics. I majored in mathematics. Vaughn and Hal each had a major in chemistry. Stig majored in mechanical engineering but nearing graduation he thought environmental engineering might be a better career path which would eventually warrant graduate school. It is interesting to note that all five of us had technical/scientific majors rather than majors in the arts and humanities. Bill, Vaughn, Hal, and I were the four who planned the trip before meeting Stig. We each purchased a bike over the 1971 Christmas holiday and began long distance training rides around Durham, NC, with some trips covering 50 or more miles. These practice trips helped us develop endurance and learn basic lessons such as the importance of always carrying water, tools, and a candy bar. I became so weak from hunger on one training trip that I couldn't get up off the ground and had to be rescued by a candy bar. Thereafter I lived by the motto: don't go far without a bar (of candy). Hal and Vaughn biked an ambitious 180 miles from Durham to Duke's Marine Lab in Beaufort, NC, over Spring Break. The trip back to Durham was aborted when a freak snowstorm hit parts of North Carolina with three inches of snow on March 25-26 and they returned by bus. Hal too had a near paralysis on this trip from presumed hypoglycemia (low blood sugar) confirming the need to carry a candy bar with us for revival.

Of note, Hal remembers the huge billboard, easily visible when biking into Smithfield, NC, which advertised the Ku Klux Klan. It displayed a hooded figure carrying a burning cross. It was torn down in 1977 after remaining for ten years and was well known in North Carolina. Jesse Helms was an openly anti-Civil-Rights five-term US senator from North Carolina; the Washington Post called him a "White Racist". Much of the South in 1972 wasn't welcoming for black persons or long-haired Duke graduates. The sculptures of Jefferson Davis, Robert E Lee, and Stonewall Jackson were completed at Stone Mountain, Georgia, in March 1972. In 1970 there had been a nation-wide student strike and shooting of students at Kent State University in which four students were killed. It seemed as though it wouldn't take much for a bigoted person to push a biker off the road if the bicyclist fit the appearance of Liberal. However, Duke moved forward by establishing a department of African American Studies in the early 1970s.

BRYAN SIMMONS

2021

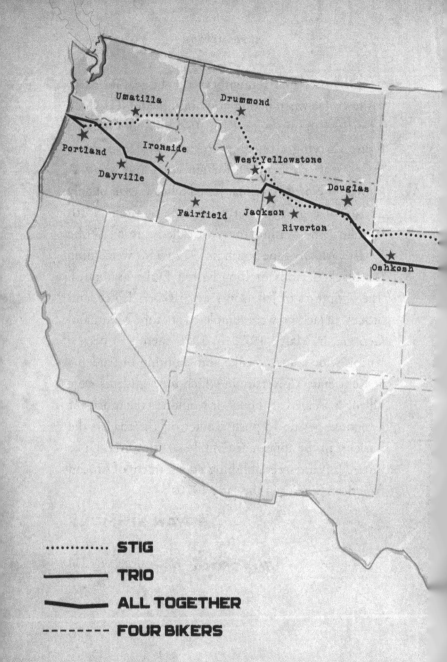

Umatilla
Drummond
Portland
Ironside
West Yellowstone
Dayville
Douglas
Fairfield
Jackson
Riverton
Oshkosh

.... STIG

———— TRIO

━━━━ ALL TOGETHER

-------- FOUR BIKERS

For more route details, see

WWW.EDMONDSPRESS.COM/THEROADTAKEN

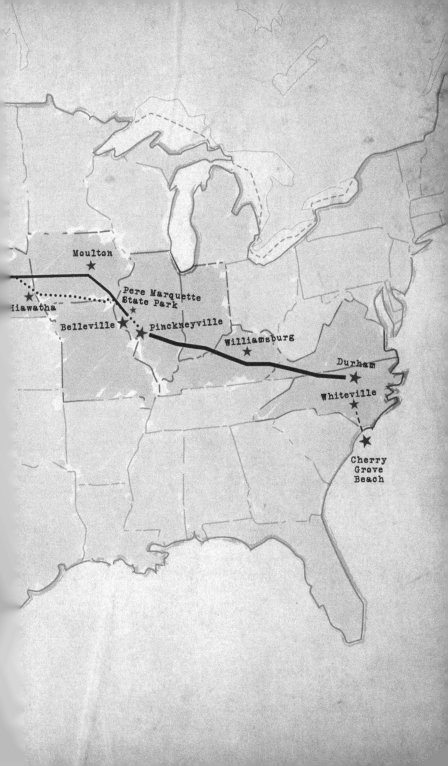

CHAPTER ONE

HATCHING THE PLAN

BRYAN

Logistics

It was, in more ways than we knew, a mammoth goal: to ride our bicycles across the United States. In the spring leading up to the odyssey, Bill, Vaughn, Hal, and I engaged in a rigorous practice schedule.

We could not find books that described how to prepare for and complete such a journey, so we had to plan and learn on our own.

Bill, our navigator, did in-depth research on the best route to take across country. We knew that we wanted to visit four places in particular: Cumberland Gap National Historic Park at the intersection of Tennessee, Virginia, and Kentucky; Hannibal, Missouri; Yellowstone National Park in Wyoming; Portland, Oregon.

This gave Bill the rough plan that he developed into a very comprehensive and detailed itinerary, including what specific roads we should take and how to establish our daily travel goals. Our travel plans were influenced by the need to sandwich the trip in between the end of school, on the one hand, and June 18 on the other, because Vaughn started work at Duke's Marine Lab the next day.

We planned to avoid big cities, unnecessary mountains, and interstate highways (where bicycles were prohibited). We needed to cross the Allegheny, Rocky, and Coastal Mountains, but there were plenty of local mountains in the West that we didn't yet know existed. One of our better ideas was to progress from the Southeast to the Northwest as we rode on into June, so we could try to avoid the high daily temperatures that the impending summer would surely bring. This was, of course, decades before we had GPS on our cellphones. Instead, Bill had an odometer fitted on his bike that was accurate when correlated with distances calculated from a map.

We decided not to carry our meals. Eating at restaurants or buying ready-to-eat foods as we went would decrease the weight we carried on our bicycles through avoiding carrying cooking equipment. We figured we would also save on food prep time so we could make better progress on our journey. My bicycle weighed 35 pounds, which is a little heavy for a touring bicycle — especially when compared to today's lightweight bicycle construction. We carried sleeping bags, but no tents, and only two sets of clothes. Even though that meant frequent visits to a laundromat, we expected the lightweight provisions would help us make good time.

We had no escort vehicle or back-up automobile. We were entirely on our own, with no one monitoring our progress by cellphone or email. We would touch base with infrequent pay-phone calls and through letters we sent by U.S. mail. We carried water, snacks, toiletries, ground cloths, tools, and bicycle/tire repair kits. Bill carried a film camera (no digital cameras yet!) and took about 50 photos that have since faded but nonetheless act as reminders of our journey. Except for a water bottle carried on the bicycle frame, our baggage was carried on the back of our bicycles, which increased the bicycle stability compared to carrying on the front. My load weighed 15 pounds on average, not including water.

An Unexpected Companion

As we were training that spring, Stig became aware of our plans serendipitously through a mutual friend six weeks before the trip was to begin. After sharing aspirations for the trip and becoming acquainted with each other, Stig asked to join our group. We all agreed with the proviso that we would leave Stig if he couldn't keep up with us.

Stig's mother had been against him embarking on a long solo bicycle trip, even though she herself had taken a tandem bicycle trip through Europe with a girlfriend when she was in her twenties. Bicycling with four other Duke graduates was a way of assuaging his mother's concerns. Stig was committed to joining the other four. However, he didn't have the benefit of the training we had been engaging in and would only later fully realize the obstacles that he would have to overcome.

CHAPTER TWO

GRADUATION PLAYS A ROLE

BRYAN

Graduation Reveling

All five bikers were graduating from Duke University in Durham, NC, and needed to organize our trip around the graduation date: May 14,1972. There was about a week between final exams and graduation, so all of us, except Stig, decided to extend our training by riding from Durham to Myrtle Beach, SC, where a large group of friends were reveling. We went swimming in the Atlantic Ocean; the movie *Jaws* was three years in the future so none of us was afraid to swim.

We mostly relaxed to recover from the stress of final exams, but we also planned our final strategy for our journey mostly by informal conversations with our friends. No one got drunk because we were not big drinkers. In my freshman year at Duke, I once got drunk and attempted to climb into a third-floor window from a second-floor roof and fell one floor. I strained muscles in my back causing severe pain that landed me in the Emergency Room with oral narcotics and rest orders. My pain didn't end with the fall though: I had decided to use a heating pad on the high setting to make the pain tolerable. Use of the high setting felt good initially but caused a second-degree burn with painful blisters on my back. I learned my lesson and never got drunk again in college.

The trip to the beach was over 176 miles but presented no problems. This leg of the trip was not considered part of the cross-country trip, but the return trip starting May 10 was included.

DAY 1:

May 10: At the Beginning

On May 10, 1972, we began our trip at 3:30 in the afternoon from Cherry Grove Beach, SC, with about a dozen friends from Duke's Southgate Dormitory there to see us off. Bill, Vaughan, Hal, and I touched the Atlantic Ocean with our hands and feet to signify the start of our planned ocean to ocean journey. As I remember that day, I felt great anxiety about completing the journey ahead of us. I wondered if we had promised much more than we could deliver.

We rode on the right-side road stripe. On that first day, I watched it too closely, so I didn't observe the scenery around us. By staying far to the right side of the road, we allowed traffic to pass us and reduced the risk of being hit by a car. It took me a while to learn to automatically follow the right sided road stripe and observe the scenery, people, and towns that we passed.

Initially, I was irritated by the traffic which passed by us in the same direction because it came so close to me. My reflexes and observations were not automatic yet, so I concentrated on looking for conditions that might make me crash or get injured. There were so many things to consider as we rode out of South Carolina that I don't remember much except my efforts to avoid injury and getting the milage completed as if I had a mundane job to do.

Stig did not bike from Cherry Grove Beach due to his own graduation activities. It was relatively uneventful, but Bill had his first flat tire and four broken spokes to repair. We stopped just north of Whiteville, NC, after traveling 45 miles and spent the night in a nearly completed home after eating dinner at Hardees. The night was uncomfortably chilly. *Cherry Grove, SC, to Whiteville, NC, 45 miles.*

DAY 2:

May 11: Our First 100 Mile Day

On May 11, Thursday, we awoke to cool crisp air and then traveled 131 miles to Duke University in Durham. We ate breakfast in Bladenboro, NC, at a dingy restaurant where we were treated like royalty. A large crowd of interested patrons were eager to hear our story. We had accomplished so little of our journey at that point that our discussions were about future plans. The patrons gave their own opinions about how to finish our journey. I could tell that some patrons envied us because of the challenge we were undertaking.

No one discouraged us. However, perhaps to scare us, someone brought up the topic of the "Beast of Bladenboro", a mysterious creature that had savaged dogs and livestock from 1953-54. More recently, the 2008 History Channel series Monster Quest concluded that the attacker might have been a cougar, but we didn't know what to think back then.

We were only charged one dollar apiece for breakfast because the restaurant owner wanted to encourage us on our trip. We then pedaled to Fayetteville where we ate lunch at the Tastee Freeze. We ate supper in Fuquay-Varina at Hardees. When leaving town, we got some angry catcalls from a driver who didn't want us on the road interfering with traffic. We did not respond to aggressive and negative comments from drivers because we feared they might retaliate against us with, what in later years would be called, road rage.

We mostly traveled on quieter highways, which Bill had purposefully integrated into our travel itinerary. I watched my fellow bikers for evidence that they might be having second thoughts about the journey, but everyone was enthusiastic. We biked 75 miles after 2:30 PM because we wanted to sleep in our dormitory beds one last time, and because we were running out of pocket money. We had only two dollars among us, including travelers checks, when we arrived at Duke. By covering well over 100 miles on the second day, we proved to ourselves that we were in good physical shape and that we had a reasonable plan for sleeping, eating, and resting on the journey to come.

The only real obstacle that day was that I developed severe tendonitis for the last 45 miles of this segment, which proved to be a major aggravation for the next 300 miles. The tendonitis finally resolved over time with topical and systemic anti-inflammatory medications despite the continued irritation caused by our vigorous biking. But injuries and inflamed tendons and muscles could not be rested; We had an aggressive schedule to keep. *Whiteville NC, to Duke University, Durham, NC, 131 miles.*

Money and Food

We learned we each needed about five to seven dollars a day for food (about $30-$40 in today's dollars). Really, it was a small amount given our enormous physical exertion and appetites. With all the work we were doing, we were able to eat large amounts of high calorie food, frequently including ice cream, milk shakes, stacks of pancakes, but of course also salads and vegetables. In addition, we would snack throughout the day with candy bars while biking.

We usually had to determine our day's itinerary by where we could find a restaurant for breakfast or dinner. In rare instances, like while we were in the desert later in the trip, we had to carry a ready-to-eat meal with us because there were long distances without a place to eat. We often ate outside of grocery stores by creating a peanut butter or cheese sandwich, or just eating a chunk of cheese. We carried travelers checks that we cashed for money as needed along the way.

Sometimes it was difficult finding a business willing to cash travelers checks. Credit cards had first been introduced in the 1950s but were not accepted in much of rural America, and we didn't qualify for them anyway. Since we did not want to carry large sums of cash that might attract thieves, we used the traveler's checks.

Developing A Pattern

Throughout the trip we rested about two to three hours at lunchtime and had brief rest stops every 10-15 miles. We tried to cover up to 60 miles before our lunch/midday break. During our lunch breaks we would often take a nap, write postcards detailing our day's travel, explore the local area, and repair bikes as needed.

Our midday breaks also allowed us to escape the most intense heat and sunlight. I, Bryan, get a sunburn very rapidly when my skin is exposed to the midday sun so had to wear full-length pants to cover as much exposed skin as possible. Effective commercial sunscreens were available as early as the 1950s, but the Sun Protection Factor (SPF) rating system was not available until 1974 — two years after our trip — and demonstrated that the early sunscreens were weak (SPF 2). The other bikers usually were able to use short pants, which I suspect were much more comfortable on hot, humid, and sunny days than what I had to wear.

I usually used the midday break to write about the day's journey, giving a detailed account on a postcard to my mother. There was so much to tell that I used micrographia, very small letters and words. We only used a campfire twice on the whole trip, both times at a designated campground at Moran Junction near Yellowstone.

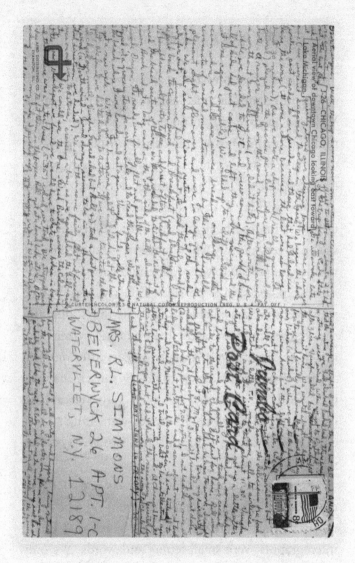

A postcard for one day that was
sent by Bryan to his mother. Note
the small lettering to cram as much
information in as possible.

A Noteworthy Graduation

We spent three days at Duke, May 12-14, attending graduation and celebrations with family members on a rainy Mother's Day. Walter Cronkite, the famed television journalist, was the keynote speaker at our graduation. I was in awe of Walter Cronkite because for years I had religiously watched his television news broadcast, which he always ended with the signature sign off "That's the way it is on Sunday, May 14, 1972" (with the date adjusted, of course).

That year Clarence Newsome became the first black student to give Duke's commencement address and later became a Baptist preacher, president of Shaw University, president of the National Underground Railroad Freedom Center in Cincinnati, and Trustee of the Duke Endowment. Terry Sanford, who had been governor of North Carolina and was a two-time US Presidential candidate, was President of Duke (1969-85) at the time. Sanford was later a U.S. Senator from 1986-93.

Family and Motivation

My mother and sisters attended the ceremony. To celebrate graduation, I probably sampled from 12 bottles of wine, donated by a Duke friend whose father was experimenting with the taste of various wines from his winery. The various wines were distinguished from each other by a letter title, such as wine "K". Without thinking of the consequences, I did this on the night before we were to continue our cross-country trip. For the first time since my freshman year, consuming too much alcohol once again burned a painful memory into my brain.

My parents had divorced just after my freshman year at Duke. I then lived with my mother in the summer and worked construction jobs as a laborer and union member near Albany, New York. Joining the union was difficult to do for students who were just working in the summer, but I did, and made an effort to show my worth by doing my share of dirty work that other workers preferred not to do.

My mother always believed in me and was confident that I could finish the trip. My father, who couldn't attend the graduation ceremony, doubted that I would finish. I had grown apart from my father and there was limited communication. I'm glad that we developed a close friendship in later years, but at the time my father did not believe in me and concluded that I could not complete such an arduous journey. This opinion drove me to succeed and was a strong incentive to continue pressing forward when the rigors of the trip were overwhelming.

CHAPTER THREE

THE ODYSSEY
BEGINS FOR ALL

BRYAN

DAY 3:

May 15: Rain, Pain, and
Political Uncertainty

On May 15, I woke up regretting that I had enjoyed so much of the twelve bottles of wine. I had a major hangover and headache when we got up at 5:45 to continue the trip. Luckily, I was not vomiting but my nausea continued for hours until my hangover resolved. My family and Bill's family were there to see us off at 7 AM. And, Stig joined us for the first time.

When we departed from Southgate dormitory, we knew we were in for a truly great adventure. However, the first day we were all together was memorable only for the rain and pain. We had breakfast at General Sherman Restaurant in Durham and departed into a steady soaking rainfall. At first, we used plastic ponchos to keep the rain off. We soon learned that using ponchos was a worthless endeavor because water from the turning wheels was thrown upward under the poncho and onto our clothing. Also, the tremendous energy exertion of cycling caused profuse sweating that soaked what clothing was otherwise dry, because sweat was trapped under the poncho. We removed the ponchos.

The biking was miserable, and this was a rough introduction to our journey for Stig. We traveled from Durham to Hillsborough to Greensboro, where we ate lunch at the Apple Restaurant. During this lunch break, Stig added a rear carrier frame to support the load he had been carrying in his backpack — good thing, too: this alleviated Stig's severe back pain.

Just after lunch, we heard about the assassination attempt on Governor George Wallace by Arthur Bremer. Wallace was a candidate for President of the United States who ran on a platform of racial segregation. Bremer also had plans to assassinate then-President Richard Nixon but was arrested before he could try. There were fears of racial and student conflict that were not comforting as we were heading into remote areas of the deep South.

For our part, we concentrated on the job at hand, long-distance biking. Due to lack of an alternate route, we were forced to travel on the interstate for five miles before we reached Winston-Salem, near Wake Forest University, but were not stopped by the highway patrol. We ate supper at a Hardees restaurant there. We preferred to eat at franchise restaurants, since we would know what to expect, but they were not available in most of rural America at the time of our journey.

My knee was again very painful at times and I took a fall from my bike after running into Stig's rear tire. I feared that the knee injury would cause me to withdraw from the trip, but determination pushed me onward, and some liniment really reduced the pain. Stig had even worse pains in his legs from muscle cramps that made it difficult to walk and sleep.

After all that had happened that day, we stopped three miles short of our planned destination, the Yadkin River, and spent the night at Vienna, NC, in a Methodist Church pavilion. We were a bit weary from our day's travel, the rain, and the pain. Throughout our journey, we slept in any convenient place, especially if it protected us from the rain and morning dew. Morning dew was not an apocalyptic catastrophe (apologies to the Grateful Dead), but it frequently soaked our sleeping bags, which then had to be air dried during our lunch break. *Durham, NC, to Vienna, NC, 96.8 miles.*

DAY 4:

May 16: Stig Sticks with It

On May 16, Bill got up at 5:15. Bill was our morning alarm clock; getting an early start was critical, and we were riding at 6:30. We ran into heavy fog at the Yadkin River, which alerted us to avoid camping in low areas near a river in the future. We ate breakfast in Yadkinville at Adams Restaurant, where a dish of brains and eggs was on the menu. None of us ordered this protein rich combination.

We ended up meeting a reporter for the local paper who wrote about our trip in The Yadkin Ripple newspaper and, in a really kind gesture, he sent copies of the article, including a group picture, to us through our parents.

We all ceremoniously mailed our first postcards at the Yadkinville post office. Lunch was near Wilkesboro where we took a break. Bill repaired his spokes, and Hal and Stig took a dip in a cold mountain stream. The day was hot and humid when we climbed a tremendous hill on US 421. We climbed an estimated 2,000 feet in 4.5 miles of winding, steep road to the Blue Ridge Parkway at the summit. The climb was extremely challenging because of the blazing sun, steep grade (7-8% maximum), and our inexperience with such demanding biking.

They're On Their Way To The Pacific

Yadkinville was a port of call Tuesday morning for an unusual group of cyclists who are on an unusual mission -- to ride their bikes completely across the United States. The five, who graduated from Duke University Sunday, began training for the stint early this year. They began their trek at the ocean at Myrtle Beach last week, stopped at Duke for their degrees Sunday, and plan to pedal to the Pacific Ocean at Astoria, Oregon, camping along the way. They travelled 100 miles Monday before stopping here for breakfast at Adams Restaurant Tuesday. Pictured are Vaughn Lamb, Southern Pines; Bryan Simmons, Watervliet, N. Y.; Hal Hemme, Youngstown, N.Y.; Bill Jackson, Chardon, Ohio; and Stig Regli, Palm Beach, Fla. They expect to make the trip in four or five weeks. Three of them plan to enter medical school this fall.

The Yadkin Ripple newspaper
reported on the riders trip West.

We learned to sneak water during a climb but never dismounted, except for Stig. He had to dismount because of his lack of physical conditioning and his inexperience with changing gears while climbing. Stig ultimately had to push his bike up this hill for about a mile. He finally caught up with us as we entered Boone, NC, about ten miles after the hill. To compensate for his inexperience, Stig began to leave early from rest breaks and let the other riders catch up. He preferred this method to falling behind and having to catch up.

We ate dinner at the student union of Appalachian State University. Here we met, by serendipity, two girls who had been Vaughn's classmates in high school. We spent the night in North Carolina behind a church near the Tennessee state line. *Vienna, NC, to TN-NC state line, 95.3 miles.*

DAY 5:

May 17: Three States in a Day

On May 17, we got started by 6:30 AM. We ate breakfast in Mountain City, TN, which was enveloped in fog, and then climbed the road to Iron Mountain. This climb included four miles of steep road with switchbacks. Maybe we should have known better, but we were surprised at the steep roads and switchbacks so early in the trip.

We then went through Shady Valley, before another two-mile climb. We stopped at South Holston Lake for skinny dipping, a bath, and shave. Bathing in cold mountain lakes and streams was invigorating and memorable. We had lunch at a grocery store and did our laundry in Bristol, on the Tennessee-Virginia border.

We were now visiting a new state every few miles. We then traveled to Kingsport, VA arriving at 5 PM. We ate supper at 6:30 PM near Natural Tunnel, a massive naturally formed cave in Virginia that is used as a railroad tunnel. We had another steep climb between Duffield and Stickleyville, VA, and camped there for the night. Most of the biking after dinner that day was either downhill or easy, so we traveled for long distances at 20 mph and exceeded our daily travel goal of 76 miles. It was a delightful day with comparatively little climbing, beautiful scenery, and good weather. *NC-TN state line to Stickleyville, VA, 98.1 miles.*

DAY 6:

May 18: A Bad Wobble and Being Unwelcome

On May 18, we awoke with our sleeping bags wet from fog and dew and started biking at daybreak. A wet sleeping bag was a big problem. The moisture interferes with sleep and it can greatly increase the weight of a bag, and neither of those were good for our progress. A wet bag was usually dried in the midday sun during a break — if it wasn't raining.

That morning, we immediately climbed a mountain reaching the 2284-foot summit. Conquering these small mountains was quite satisfying but we knew the Rockies would be a much greater challenge, and they lingered large in our imaginations.

We reached Jonesville for breakfast at 7:30, and then climbed steadily following the route traveled by Daniel Boone (now US 58) into Kentucky. Boone's was a name we recognized — an archetypal frontier hero of American folklore.

We arrived at the Cumberland Gap National Historical Park at 11 AM. The scenery was spectacular. The Gap is at 1648 feet altitude and led us into Kentucky, my birthplace.

The Gap was the first big goal of our trip. Using the Cumberland Gap allowed us to minimize the number of mountains we would have to climb early on our journey. The Gap had great historical significance for all of us, as well as being a landmark of visual beauty.

We ate lunch at Jerry's Restaurant north of Middlesboro, KY, before proceeding toward Pineville where we took a rest. Stig resumed biking early to get a lead but got into an accident with a paperboy. He collided with such force that he was concerned of having caused significant injury. Fortunately, the paperboy seemed OK and disappeared quickly to complete his paper delivery. Our group had not anticipated such a collision, and it expanded our understanding of what could go wrong on a bicycle journey.

The Cumberland Gap is a natural passage from the East into Kentucky. For 150 years after the first settlements in Virginia, the forbidding Alleghenies kept the English colonists from Kentucky. Indians were aware of the Gap but, until 1750, the colonists were not. Soon after the colonists discovered this passage, hunting parties started to enter Kentucky, including those led by Daniel Boone. Boone should not be confused with Davy Crockett who was raised near the Gap but was 52 years younger than Boone. At one point in 1775, there were plans to name the newly discovered land "Transylvania." During the Revolutionary War, The Gap allowed soldiers of the rebellion to capture important British forts near the Ohio River. Most importantly, the Gap allowed the trans-Allegheny migration to extend the western boundary of the United States to the Mississippi River.

Stig's front wheel was severely distorted and needed to be replaced because, even with attempts to straighten it, the tire wobbled and rubbed against the brakes and frame. He could only use his rear brake which would be dangerous if braking at high speeds. There was no bicycle shop in town, or any other place along the route, until just outside St. Louis, MO, that had a replacement wheel, so we had to continue with Stig riding a wobbly bike for hundreds of miles.

Stig had extraordinary tenacity because he was the least prepared biker, yet he continued onward with what, fortunately, turned out to be the most serious bicycle problem of the trip. As we turned onto route KY 92 five miles beyond Pineville, we realized the area was desolate and for some reason or another seemed unfriendly to us.

Except for our group, young college students were nowhere to be found. We stopped at one of the few stores we encountered and noticed a man leaning up against his car staring menacingly at us, perhaps thinking we were long-haired trespassers. He seemed to be trying to send a hostile message and we got it.

We were afraid to stop anywhere nearby and continued to Williamsburg, KY. Hal remembers that the same man on a motorcycle passed us several times, as if we were under surveillance; however, nothing but our own anxiety came from this concern. We ate supper there and then began searching for a safe place to sleep. We eventually slept beside a Baptist Church four miles northwest of Williamsburg.

During this day, Stig played a prank on Vaughn. Vaughn was a very competitive cyclist and would catch up to Stig in a fairly short time, even though Stig left rest stops early to get a head start, which negated Stig's reason for leaving early. During the afternoon break, Stig left early but soon hid behind some trees and let Vaughn go racing past him. Stig then followed Vaughn, who kept a fast pace trying to catch up to Stig, who he thought was ahead of him. Finally, after about 30 minutes, Vaughn pulled his bike over on the side of the road and waited only to find Stig unexpectedly behind him. Stig told Vaughn he had pulled off the road for a snack, which he did, even though that was not his primary motivation. He never told Vaughn about his prank, but his satisfaction outweighed his guilt. It was not the last prank of the journey but was probably the most audacious. Despite being a stranger, Stig fit well into the group. *Stickleyville, VA, to Williamsburg, KY, 106.9 miles.*

DAY 7:

May 19: Mud and Repairs

On May 19, we started at 7:30 and quickly encountered fog, which was even more dangerous for us than cars.

We did not want to end up bonded with someone's front fender. We had no lights or means of alerting drivers to our presence. We just tried to stay out of the way of cars.

Vaughn had a flat tire that, after patching, went flat again. He replaced the tube with a spare. In addition, Hal's derailleur broke and took 20 minutes to fix. A derailleur is a gear changing mechanism usually near the rear wheel hub. We lost a lot of time with these repair delays but reached Cumberland Falls by 10:30. We visited the museum quickly because we hadn't eaten breakfast yet. We ate at a motel restaurant near the Falls and then headed for Burnside, KY, where we found the General Burnside Island State Park and Lake Cumberland. Ambrose Burnside was a Union general during the Civil War. His distinctive style of facial hair became known as sideburns after his last name.

We stopped to rest and bathe. It started to rain, and we were soaked, but lunch at a nearby restaurant served to kill time until the rain stopped. I always worried when we stopped for rain, unless it was a downpour, because it could rain for hours and get us seriously behind schedule. It stopped raining at 3:30 PM and we resumed travel to Somerset. Mud was thrown up onto our clothes from the churning wheels. Being covered in mud limited the options for eating at a restaurant many times throughout the journey. Getting muddy could also mean that you would be muddy for several days if a bath, a change of clothing, and/or a laundromat were not conveniently available. We tried hard to not look like dirty bums. This also required shaving frequently with a sharp razor and soap lubricant. We were reluctant to bike on the wet road surface fearing that it was dangerously slippery, but we biked anyway because we had a schedule to keep.

We rode across the Eastern Time Zone boundary to Russell Springs where we ate at Smith's Steak House. Despite the restaurant's name, we ordered the all-you-can-eat fish special for $1.25. We slept in the playgrounds behind an elementary school, a decision that would probably get us arrested today.

Williamsburg, KY, to Russell Springs, KY, 84.8 miles.

I discovered a broken spoke but waited to fix it because the bike could easily function normally with one spoke missing, and the repair is very complicated and time consuming. The repair requires removing the tire, tube, and old spoke, then inserting a new one. The new spoke then has to be tightened skillfully and symmetrically to keep the tire centered without any wobble when the wheel is turning.

Counting Time and Physical Cost

Clock time was not as important to us as daylight time. We sometimes would travel late into the evening because there was still daylight and we needed to make up for lost time due to accidents, flat tires, bike problems, and hard rain. Generally, Bill had us up and going at daylight or before, but we usually stopped for the day well before dark. In the middle of the day, wrist watches allowed us to determine if we were maintaining schedule. We probably spent 8-12 hours per day on the bicycles, with the longest hours in Nebraska and Idaho where we battled headwinds estimated at 15-20 miles per hour.

Spending 8-12 hours a day on a bicycle for over a month caused pain and discomfort that wasn't always anticipated. At the beginning of the trip, sitting on the narrow, hard bicycle seats caused a bruise-like pain in the groin and buttocks. Within a week or so, this pain disappeared. Pedaling caused tendonitis and muscle pain in the legs, especially since there was very little time to rest the tendon or muscle. I had pain in my legs at the end of the day which I later learned was due to mild restless leg syndrome (RLS), which is now severe. Having severe RLS would make it very unlikely that I could repeat this journey now. The touring bikes that we used had a "U" shaped front handlebar that gave the option to use the upper or lower grip. Using the lower grip caused the biker to lean forward into an aerodynamic position but it put more weight on the hands. This caused nerve injury with pain and tingling of the fingers. Use of padded gloves can limit this hand nerve injury.

Falls from the bikes were a significant risk because all five of us used toe clips. Toe clips are a cage-like enclosure on the pedal that allows the biker to lift as well as depress the pedal. The clips markedly increase pedaling efficiency when climbing a hill or battling severe wind drag. The danger is that when the clips are snug, they trap the foot and prevent the rider from rapidly dismounting the bike to prevent a fall. Today's rapid-attach shoes and pedals allow for a quicker and safer breakaway in case of falls.

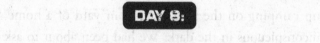

May 20: Hospitality?

On May 20, we were up before 6 AM and in Columbia, KY, for breakfast at the Circle R Restaurant by 6:30. We then biked to Greensburg and Munfordville. We ate lunch and, for the second time, did our laundry. Washing and drying our clothes usually took several hours and so we only did this during long breaks. We arrived in Leitchfield for supper at the Old West

Steak House, where I ordered a steak. Leitchfield was named for an aide to General George Washington, Major David Leitch. We took time to make our first phone calls home. We ran into a judge who offered to let us stay in the jail voluntarily as free lodging, but we would be near several convicted murderers and therefore we declined.

The tradition of free lodging in jail has apparently ended but was prevalent at the time of our journey. We slept in jail voluntarily several times as a place to escape the weather and get a mattress. Luckily, bed bugs were not a problem. Each jail had its own rules, but generally anyone who slept voluntarily in jail had to surrender anything that might be used to injure anyone. We were not sure if the judge had a plan to rid the world of several long haired, hippie lookalikes. So, with darkness closing in, we sprinted four miles out of town. We ended up camping on the very large front yard of a home, inconspicuous in the dark. We had been about to ask permission to stay beside a Fundamentalist Church, but a revival meeting was in progress and we preferred sleep as a method of revival for ourselves. *Russell Springs, KY, to Leitchfield, KY, 100.7 miles.*

Boredom

Our moods were greatly influenced by the beauty, or lack thereof, of the countryside. The heat, rain, loneliness, extreme exertion, and long hours in the saddle were taxing. It was almost impossible to have an interesting conversation when we were traveling one behind the other, especially if there was busy traffic. It was all worth the effort when gorgeous scenery was the reward. Unfortunately, much of southern Kentucky had monotonous rolling hills devoid of interesting features, unlike northern Kentucky, where I was born in Lexington. Such uninspiring scenery in southern Kentucky lowered all our moods, especially Hal's. Good conversation was the only other antidote to boredom, and most of this took place when we were eating our meals.

May 21: Inspiration

On May 21, Sunday, we were riding by 5:45 AM but had to travel 25 miles for breakfast in Fordsville. Lunch was in Sorgho at a grocery store. Grocery stores provided candy bars, inexpensive sandwiches, peanut butter, drinks, sometimes air conditioning, shelter, and rapid service. The temperature was above 96 degrees, the highest of the trip, and extremely uncomfortable. We did not get visible perspiration when we were biking at high speeds because sweat would evaporate, but when we stopped, we could become quickly drenched in sweat if it was hot and humid and we had exerted ourselves.

We ended up on a toll road, the Audubon Highway for four miles, before we realized bikes were prohibited. We left the highway by passing our bikes over a fence to use a local road; we had to pass the bicycles back over the fence when the new road came to a dead end. The highway was named after the ornithologist, naturalist, and painter Audubon, who lived in Henderson, KY from 1810-1819.

We biked into Henderson where we took a long afternoon break, hoping the temperature would drop. We left Henderson at 4:30 PM after each devouring a banana split. We then traveled to Morganfield, where we ate at a local popular diner, eating our first and last pizza of the trip. Pizza restaurants were just not common on our route, especially in rural areas. The local youth were very interested in our adventure, and some even followed us out of town. I was taken aback when the high school students were so interested in our journey that they wanted a prolonged conversation. We took time to answer questions from the students and explain why we voluntarily accepted the challenge of the vigorous journey. Surprisingly, we were beginning to see the rewards of the trip were more than just meeting the challenge. We were learning so much about our country and, perhaps, inspiring others to set ambitious goals. I would not be surprised if someone we met from Morganfield took a long journey by bicycle. We stopped for the night at the intersection of KY 56 and 109 and slept in a freshly cut field. *Leitchfield, KY, to intersection KY 56 and 109, 109 miles.*

Judging Safety

Intermittently, we would worry about our safety, especially while riding on narrow highways, and during sleep when we had no shelter. Large 18-wheelers would pass us on a two-lane highway at what seemed to be 60 miles per hour (mph) or more. Some would even blast their horns purposefully to scare us. Trucks came so close that we could feel the tug of the truck's vacuum after it passed. We had to develop nerves of steel and steer our bicycles so steadily that we could keep the front tire within the right painted stripe. Until we got further west, it was impossible to avoid the busy two-lane highways. Some individuals yelled and gestured at us, but this was infrequent. Perhaps the greatest danger was that we wore no helmets and sometimes traveled 50 mph down steep mountain roads later in the trip. We fell and hit our heads several times but fortunately these occurred at low speed and did no serious brain damage (at least that is our story). Using bicycle helmets would have lowered the risk of head injury by 50%, but helmet use was not common in

1972. Bicycles were mostly considered safe toys rather than a potentially dangerous means of long-distance transportation. We feared trespassing on private property and angering the owner. So, when possible, we asked permission to sleep on private property. Wild animals were never a problem. We were never armed, not even with a substantial knife.

DAY 10:

May 22: Unexpected Plans for Separation

On May 22, we were up before 6 AM. We slept poorly because we were camping at the intersection of two busy highways. Trucks kept stopping and shifting gears and accelerating all night long. We crossed the Ohio River into Illinois on the Shawneetown Bridge. Although the bridge had a toll, we avoided paying it because we failed to trip the vehicle counter. We ate breakfast in Shawneetown, six miles up the road. "Old" Shawneetown had been on the river but was destroyed by flooding and the new city moved to its current location.

While on the way to Eldorado, IL, Stig had a flat tire that took some time to repair because he accidentally re-inserted the leaking tube instead of the replacement. In Eldorado, Vaughn, Hal, and I picked up some mail, using one of several pre-arranged pickup points for the trip. This mail arrangement worked well but sometimes we arrived on a Sunday when the post office was closed or, alternatively, the letter had been mailed but not yet received by the post office.

We ate lunch in Benton from a grocery store. Benton was home to Beatles' member George Harrison's sister, Louise. George visited her in 1963, the first visit from a member of the rock group to America.

Hal was dealing with aching joints and a headache. When we resumed biking after lunch, Stig had another flat tire and had to return to Benton for repairs. The rest of us continued on to Bend Lake for a swim and a bath. Bathing was done generally by skinny dipping in remote areas in lakes and streams or occasionally in shower houses at public parks. No one was ever discovered naked and arrested. We each had soap and a small towel.

It was here that Hal announced that he would be going home once he reached St. Louis. He was understandably bored and figured he could at least get paid to be bored at home, and he needed the money because he was about to enter medical school. In addition, the outside temperature was almost intolerable that day at 96 degrees. The rest of our group was shocked and disappointed because Hal was a great companion with an excellent sense of humor, but we couldn't change Hal's mind despite our best attempts. We all had a large chicken supper at Luke's Place in Pinckneyville, near where we camped for the night. Pinckneyville was a "sundown town" from 1890 to 1968, which meant for Black Americans "don't let the sun go down with you still in the city or else."[1] We saw several active and inactive oil wells that evening. Unfortunately, we camped out under a tree full of young caterpillars that rained down upon us all night long. The juicy crushed caterpillar bodies littered our sleeping bags in the morning. When the first caterpillars fell, we would slap our faces when a caterpillar landed there, thinking it was some large biting insect. We quickly learned not to do this. We could have just moved from under the tree but moving required too much effort in the darkness of the middle of the night. Sleep was extremely important, and we avoided anything that disturbed it. *Highway intersection 56 and 109, KY, to Pinckneyville, IL, 93.1 miles.*

CHAPTER FOUR

SEPARATION ANXIETY

BRYAN

DAY 11:

May 23: St. Louis and Farewell

On May 23, we had breakfast at 6:30 AM in Coulterville. We then rode 45 miles to Belleville, IL, by 10:30 to get Stig a new wheel at a comprehensive bike shop. This also allowed Stig to join an old friend from the Duke golf team (Eric Weidmann) who lived there. Hal left the group in Belleville to join his grandfather who lived in St. Louis. Of note, his grandfather was unexpectedly in the hospital but released soon after. Hal was someone special to me. Hal was my roommate for three of my four years at Duke and was the one who convinced me to prepare for and apply to medical school. He changed my life and seeing him leave was not easy.

Bill, Vaughn, and I worked on our bikes outside the bike shop; Bill described the repairs as a needed major overhaul. Spokes were replaced, and ball bearings were repacked. Stig planned to stay in Belleville for the night and join us 130 miles away the next day in Hannibal, Missouri. We calculated that this goal would give Stig time to catch up with the trio if he was determined.

The three remaining riders left Stig and decided to avoid St. Louis by remaining in Illinois to bypass the busy bridges and roads that surround the city. This detour was by far the greatest deviation from our planned route as determined by Bill before we started our trip. His planning was almost perfect because we bikers used the pre-selected roads throughout the trip, with few exceptions, and without problems. Any decision to change our route and other changes and disagreements were resolved through discussion. The most important conversations were how and when to change our itinerary, such as using a route that was not planned. Bill always took the lead in these discussions because he had the maps and odometer, and he was so reasonable.

We traveled through East St. Louis, where we caught a glimpse of the Gateway Arch in St. Louis. The heavy traffic and many potholes made it the worst road of the trip. Potholes cause a bumpy ride. I began to think that deviating from our original route was a mistake. We did stop in Freeburg for an ice cream cone and saw the Annual Freeburg Grade School Parade. We finally saw the Mississippi River, a major landmark of the trip, as we headed north after Freeburg. The river was gorgeous and alive with river traffic.

I yearned to arrive in Hannibal and visit the museum of steamboat captain and author Mark Twain. We continued to Grafton, IL, on a divided highway, cooled by the river on our left, with high bluffs on our right. We ate dinner and then camped in a picnic pavilion at Pere Marquette State Park. We used the showers to clean up; the mosquitoes liked us anyway and were the worst of the trip. Dogs barking and thunder also disturbed our sleep. *Pinckneyville, IL, to Pere Marquette State Park, IL, 102.6 miles.*

The Mighty Mississippi

The Mississippi River was well known to me from living in Memphis, TN, but it was new to Bill and Vaughn. Many bridges that go across the river are also interstate highways, so we had to carefully select our point of crossing, which we eventually determined would be the bridge crossing to Hannibal. The river itself is over 2000 miles long, and it also connected with the Missouri River at St. Louis to drain most of the land we covered on our journey. It drains all or part of 32 states between the

Appalachian and Rocky Mountains. Its name comes from the Native American Ojibwe Tribe who called the river "Messipi" which means "Big River" or "Father of Waters." The book *Rising Tide: The Great Mississippi Flood of 1927 and How It Changed America*, by John Barry is very informative about the history, importance, and dangers of the river. There are hundreds of books, fictional and non-fictional, about the lore of this great river.[ii]

Hazards

There were many roadside hazards throughout the trip. Hitting a large pothole could very likely bend the tire rim and break spokes. Water-drainage grates at the edge of the road could easily trap a tire and catapult the rider into the street. Cars and trucks parked by the road sometimes had drivers that suddenly opened their doors and presented a dangerous barrier unless the biker was ready to stop instantly or veer left into traffic. If it rained on a muddy or oily road, it could be quite slippery. And narrow roads full of traffic would often

force us onto the shoulder where a drop-
off could cause us to fall. Anticipating
these hazards became second nature by
the time we were in MO.

DAY 12:

May 24: Deepening Discouragement

On May 24, we took the Scenic River Route following the Mississippi River to Hardin, IL, where we crossed the Illinois River and ate breakfast. We then traveled 57 miles before lunch in Rockport, IL. Mr. Browning, the restaurant proprietor, was interested in our trip and took pictures of us that he mailed to our homes. Rockport was one of the best stops of the journey because of the excitement caused by discussions of our trip. Rockport was a small, unincorporated township, but it had at least one busy restaurant that day. We then rode to a rest area along Illinois route 96 for our afternoon break. When we resumed our travel westward, we encountered our first strong westerly wind and it slowed us considerably.

We crossed the Mississippi River at Hannibal, MO, at 5 PM. We found the Mark Twain Museum had just closed. We peered into the windows of his home and read the historical markers. Hannibal was the second major planned landmark goal, after Cumberland Gap, because all of us loved the literary works of Mark Twain. Hannibal is best known as the 19th-century boyhood home of Samuel Langhorne Clemens, best known as Mark Twain. The exploits of Twain's fictional characters, Tom Sawyer and Huckleberry Finn, were inspired by life in Hannibal. For our trio, it also signaled that we had completed one-third of our trip, after covering over 1,000 miles. By the time we got past the Mississippi River, we were able to maintain speeds of 20 mph through gentle hills and with minimal headwinds for over an hour at a time.

Stig was supposed to meet us at 5 PM but he was nowhere to be found. We had a long debate about whether to wait for Stig in Hannibal, or to move on given that we had a tight schedule to maintain. We had discussed the entire planned route with Stig, so we assumed that he would know that we would head toward Palmyra where he could easily locate us. We were the only bicycle group likely to be in this small town, so the three of us pedaled to Palmyra where we ate supper and did our laundry.

Stig never appeared. We felt very bad because we thought that the failure to rendezvous with Stig was our fault. We should have remained in Hannibal, despite the tight schedule. We knew however, we would have to average over 100 miles per day to finish on time, and we were very uncertain that we could do this.

Bill Jackson rests on the boyhood home of Mark Twain.

Furthermore, we should have agreed to phone a common number for communication and new directions to meet, but we hadn't thought that would be necessary and we were wrong. Cell phones did not exist. We slept near Palmyra under an ammonia tank; anhydrous ammonia was subsequently shown to be the cause of tremendous explosions. Anhydrous ammonia is flammable, toxic by inhalation, and corrosive. It was used as the explosive agent for the Oklahoma City bombing in 1995. Even worse than sleeping under a potential bomb were the mosquitoes, which remained with us all night long.

The three of us who remained in one group (the trio) were devastated by the losses of Hal and Stig from the journey. The camaraderie the two had generated had been rewarding and was absolutely missed.

Pere Marquette State Park, IL, to Palmyra, MO, 99 miles.

However, the more riders a bicycle group has without using a following rescue/ escort vehicle, the slower the group moves because they can only travel as fast as the slowest rider. Flat tires, bent wheels, broken axles and derailleurs, and individual personal needs and maladies all slowed progress and caused boredom. The ideal number of riders for a long bike trip without an escort may be three. This is enough to assist with chores of riding such as reducing wind drag by alternating the lead and being

able to collectively make plans and help
the fellow riders while participating in
interesting conversations.

Nonetheless, we were really feeling down about what we thought was the "abandonment" of Stig. We had lost two companions within 24 hours, had missed seeing Mark Twain's house and museum by minutes, had encountered our first strong westerly wind causing significant drag, had to ride in oppressive heat and humidity, were bored by much of the monotonous scenery, and were being eaten alive by mosquitos at night. The heat at night meant that we slept mostly outside our sleeping bags, leaving much flesh and blood for the mosquitoes to attack.

I began to wonder if I could finish the transcontinental trip, or if I would be the next one to go. Certainly, completing over 1000 miles, as Hal had done, was a major accomplishment, and would allow us to quit with dignity. However, I knew my father would feel that his opinion that I couldn't complete the trip was confirmed. I think that all three of us decided that we must go on and complete the trip or we would never know what we had missed. We decided to double down on our biking and work closely together, helping each other as needed. If we were going to fail, we would go down fighting. In addition, we would do whatever we could to locate Stig and see if he continued on alone or if he was forced to quit, due to the lack of companionship and help. If he had continued on, we were determined to find him and reunite our group of bikers as we pressed on to reach the Pacific Ocean.

CHAPTER FIVE

A NEW START
FOR STIG

STIG

STIG'S DAY 12:

May 24: Breaking Away

After separating from my friends in Belleville, IL with a new front rim and functioning brakes, I cycled for about an hour before finding my friend Eric Weidmann's house at the outskirts of Belleville. After a warm welcome and shower Eric hesitatingly asked if I wanted to play a few holes of golf with him at his home course. We could do so before having dinner with his family, when his sister and father would return from work.

Eric and I had developed a deep friendship playing golf together at Duke, and even though I was tired from the long day, I could not resist this invitation. We managed to play nine holes of golf before returning for a delicious homemade meal prepared by his mom. Eric's family wanted to hear the full story of the bicycle trip and I graciously gave them a full recounting.

That night at the Weidmann's I had the best night's sleep for the entire journey. The next morning, I headed for Hannibal, MO, with a full breakfast, a fresh pair of legs, and a warm family send-off. My plan was to rendezvous with Bryan, Bill, and Vaughn at the Mark Twain Museum at 5 PM. I followed the Great River Road adjacent to the Mississippi River and made excellent time with a strong tailwind. I felt confident with an exuberant sense of freedom that I had not felt before on this trip. The scenery was historic, alive, and uplifting. Imagined impressions of life along the Mississippi River and memories of the previous days' cycling adventures flooded my mind.

Memories of inspirational searches for meaning in life, that are found in books that I had read, became as real as if I were living them. Such books included *Zorba the Greek, On The Road, The Razor's Edge, Narcissus and Goldmund,* and *Siddhartha*. My exuberance came crashing down when I hit a strong headwind approaching Hannibal and realized that I probably would not make the rendezvous. I worried about how long they might wait for me, and if they had left, how I might be able to reunite. When I arrived in Hannibal at 6 PM, my friends were nowhere to be found. I knew that they would head west, most likely by one of two routes, Palmyra, or Monroe City.

I regretted not having paid more attention to Bill's planned route beyond the immediate day at hand. With little more than two hours of sunlight remaining, I pedaled with full fury toward Monroe City, MO, hoping to catch up with them. I hoped they had taken the same route. Finally, I was overcome by hunger and stopped 15 miles west of Hannibal at a roadside diner which, much to my amazement, offered an all-you-can-eat smorgasbord.

I glared desperately through the window, wondering whether my sweaty attire would allow entry. One of the waitresses compassionately signaled for me to come in. Astonished at my good fortune, I parked my bike alongside the window of the diner, entered, and stacked my tray with an assortment of goodies, and ravenously began to eat. Shortly thereafter, a State Trooper approached me and asked if he could sit at my table. I curiously obliged. The Trooper asked if the three cyclists that he had seen heading toward Palmyra might be my friends. When I told him what had happened, the State Trooper offered to give me a ride to meet up with them.

I struggled in silence for a few moments. While I missed my companions, I also realized that the freedom I had felt riding alone along the Great Mississippi had been my most fulfilling day of the trip so far. When traveling with the group I had felt constrained by the adherence to the repetitive everyday routine of ride, eat, two-hour mid-day break, ride, eat, and sleep, mostly with specific defined time intervals for each.

I did appreciate how the disciplined structure for each day had helped group cohesion, but I hadn't realized how much I had missed spontaneous independence. Ridden with some underlying anxiety, I gratefully declined the offer from the State Trooper. I thus made the conscious decision to journey forth alone, a decision that was to have an enormous influence in what was to follow.

I would regret this decision in short order, but my impulse was to try traveling alone with the possibility that we might reunite later on. I gobbled up my remaining apple pie and ice cream and continued cycling westward on US36 with no idea where I would sleep. With night closing in, I stopped five miles short of Monroe City and found a place to sleep amidst some brush below a small bridge. Here I slept until the middle of the night, when I awoke terrified by the sound of a train approaching and passing by. It was not until morning that I realized the train tracks were within 100 feet of where I had been sleeping. *Belleville, IL, to near Monroe City, MO, 150 miles.*

STIGS DAY 13:

May 25: A Perfect Day

I woke up at dawn on May 25th inside my sleeping bag, legs now pleasantly rather than achingly sore, and grateful for the unexpected events of the previous day. And yet I wondered, as hunger set in, had I made the right decision of not accepting the ride from the State Trooper to join my friends? I knew that their next mail pickup (mine included) was in Crete, Nebraska, and that there might be a possibility of rejoining the trio, depending upon timing. Cycling in the early morning is generally the coolest part of the day, and the opportunity for potentially reconnecting with my friends provided added motivation for quickly getting on the road. Today, there was not a cloud in the sky and little wind — perfect for cycling.

After five miles I was hungry and tempted to have breakfast in Monroe City, MO, but I continued for another 18 miles to Shelbina, where I loaded up with pancakes and a mushroom omelet at a small friendly diner. I then continued west on 36W riding through mostly flat wheat, soy, and sorghum croplands. The newness of this terrain was at first interesting, but as this scenery continued for many miles, I became bored and wanted change. In the early afternoon, the monotony broke when I discovered a small lake near Westbrook and took a swim to escape the near 100-degree temperature.

That evening I found a small park in Chillicothe where I met an elderly couple, having the last name Gladieux, who invited me home for a shower and dinner.

Near Monroe City, MO, to Chillicothe, MO, 110 miles.

 Chillicothe' means big town' in Shawnee, named so in 1774. Today, Chillicothe s population is about 10,000 people, having grown about 10-fold over the last 150 years, but very little since 1970. Chillicothe is also known as The Home of Sliced Bread'. The Chillicothe Baking Company began selling pre-sliced bread in the area in 1928, marking the first time sliced bread was available commercially in the world.

STIGS DAY 14:

May 26: A Tire and Gratitude

On May 26th, following a generous breakfast and given a bag lunch to go, I set forth for St. Joseph, MO, where I hoped to find a bike shop to replace my rear tire which was wearing thin and leading to frequent punctures. I regretted not having bought new tires before we started our trip back in Durham. I had heard word of mouth that new tires with good pressure maintenance could last for about 3000 miles, which would have been well worth it.

By early afternoon, I arrived in St. Joseph where I found a bike shop with a mechanic named Tux who was servicing a college cyclist en route to Madison, Wisconsin from Albuquerque, NM. As I waited for my turn for Tux to replace my tire, I learned that the short-lived Pony Express (1860-1861) had gone through St. Joseph prior to the completion of the transcontinental railroad; and that the infamous bank and train robber, Jesse James had lived and been gunned down here in the 1880's. When I shared my journey with Tux, he told me he would like to be in my place, touring the US on a bicycle rather than repairing them. He did sell me a new rear tire. I reflected on my privilege for being able to do this trip, and soon gratefully continued westward on US36 with renewed excitement.

It was nearly 100 degrees in late afternoon when I crossed into Kansas. I soon arrived in Hiawatha, one of the earliest towns in Kansas, named after the poem, *Song of Hiawatha*, by Henry Wadsworth Longfellow. Near the roadside I heard splashing water and boisterous play coming from a nearby public pool. I checked in for a shower and swim, had a couple of burgers and a chocolate shake and, with an hour or so of daylight left, found a nearby public park and a bench on which I slept for the night encased in my sleeping bag. *Chillicothe, MO, to Hiawatha, KS, 111 miles.*

STIG'S DAY 15:

May 27: What Might Have Been, but Wasn't to Be

On May 27th I set forth for Crete, NE where I hoped to receive mail at the post office. I wondered if there might be word from Bryan, Bill, and Vaughn who were also picking up mail there. It was an overcast day until light rain fell briefly near Virginia, NE, where I stopped at a small grocery store for lunch. I chatted with a woman buying groceries and learned that milo, also known as sorghum, had replaced corn for feedstock because of crop devastation from the corn bug. I also used a payphone in the grocery store to call the post office in Crete to see if there was any mail for me. I anticipated spending the night in Crete and leaving early the next day, before the post office opened, if there was no mail for me. I felt a huge let down when I learned that no mail had come, but my spirits picked up when the rain stopped. I cycled as fast as I could, anticipating the rain might soon begin again.

As I continued, I reflected how each day had been a new adventure, not knowing what or who I might encounter or where I would eat or sleep. I experienced an added level of anxiety in traveling alone, but had a heightened alertness to what the changing surroundings might offer. For the most part, this seemed like a good tradeoff, but not during times of inclement weather or facing strong headwinds.

An extraordinary set of circumstances occurred in Crete that evening. I discovered the Doane College Women's dormitory near the center of town, but it was closed due to classes not being in session. I serendipitously met a woman named Christie, a prefect for the dormitory, who was kind enough to let me stay there for the night. As our conversation deepened and we shared our passion for golf, I learned that Christie had been a 3-time women's amateur golf champion of Nebraska. After a quick shower and homemade meal, Christie invited me to play a few holes of golf with her on the Doane College Heights Golf Course before the sun set. Afterward, back at the dorm I was served a pudding-like dessert that I was so taken by that I asked Christie for the recipe (6 egg yolks, 1/2 cup of sugar, 1/2 cup of flour, 2 tablespoons of butter; cook, and beat continuously while adding Vanilla and Kirsch). I was starting to feel smitten by Christie until she shared her excitement of getting married the next week. *Hiawatha, KS, to Crete, NE, 140 miles.*

CHAPTER SIX

THE TRIO HEADS OUT WEST WITHOUT STIG

BRYAN

THE TRIO'S DAY 13:

May 25: Headwinds

On May 25, we arose before sunrise for an early start and found a restaurant for a pancake breakfast at a Missouri Route 6 intersection. Stig still had not joined us so we inquired about a lone bicyclist, and none had been seen by those in the restaurant. We thought it likely that Stig had quit because of his poor physical conditioning and lack of companionship. We decided to keep going but left word about our planned route for that day, just in case Stig was still biking but at a slower pace.

We traveled on to Durham, Lewiston, and Edina, MO, before having lunch in Baring. We had traveled 68 miles by 1 PM when we took a long break at a roadside park. When we resumed riding, a strong westerly wind was again a major problem. We passed by Memphis, MO, and then had dinner at Lancaster, MO. The countryside was characterized by rolling hills with crops and pig farms. We then crossed into Iowa and biked into Moulton, where we stayed the night at a cemetery. We carefully selected our camp site to avoid any chance of taking up permanent residence there. This was our only night in a cemetery, and it was spooky. Certainly, there were much better places to stay. Even now, the two Moulton cemeteries don't make the list of the best places to stay nearby. *Palmyra, MO, to Moulton, IA, 113 miles.*

Headwinds

A strong headwind is a major problem for a cyclist. Wind resistance (drag) can slow the biker down dramatically. If the biker wants to maintain the same speed in the headwind it can require an enormous increase in calorie consumption. For example, if a biker wants to maintain

a speed of 15 mph when confronted
with a headwind of 15 mph, the calorie
consumption per minute would increase
about 4-fold. If the biker dropped back
in speed to 10 mph but with the same 15
mph headwind, the calorie consumption
would still increase by about two-fold.[iii]
Aerodynamic drag accounts for 70-90%
of the resistance felt when pedaling.
The only greater obstacle to resistance-
free cycling is climbing. However, when
you climb a mountain, you typically get
a payback ride downhill on the other
side. Wind drag gives you no return on
your energy investment. Another form of
resistance when biking is the friction
between the tire and the road, which can
be minimized by high-inflation-pressure
tires. This road resistance is usually
relatively minor but adds up when you
are covering long distances. We inflated
our tires at gas stations periodically
to reduce road friction. We learned
important techniques to avoid drag:

* follow closely behind the
  bicycle in front and let this
  person break the wind;

* hunker down into an
  aerodynamic position;

* and don't try to go fast
  into a steady headwind.

Headwinds were particularly bad in Nebraska, Idaho, and along the Columbia River in Washington State. In these states, it was like someone took all the winds, *except* those blowing West, and put these in an ox skin bag to impede our progress. We could avoid the worst winds by traveling early in the morning, because the winds seemed to pick up in the early afternoon. Anyone who plans to ride a bicycle cross-country should consider going from West to East, because the prevailing winds travel west to east. This would decrease, or eliminate the worst wind drag for those traveling eastward.

Even if we had known about the importance of prevailing westerly winds, we had to attend graduation near the East Coast and adhere to a tight schedule. In addition, we had not known how well we would succeed, and didn't want to start too far from home.

THE TRIO'S DAY 14:

May 26: Cookies and a Rainless Storm

On May 26, Friday, we started at sunrise and ate breakfast in Centerville, Iowa. We pushed hard to get to Mount Ayr, IA, to pick up mail before the post office closed. The outside temperature was hot and miserable, and we did a lot of sweating, which increased the need for a renewed supply of water.

We traveled Iowa Route 2 and completed 60 miles of biking by 11:30 when we had lunch in Leon. We arrived in Mount Ayr by 3:30 PM and were able to pick up Bill's mail, which included cookies! Bill shared his cookies so generously that we couldn't finish our dinner. We rested after dinner in Mount Ayr until 6 PM and then resumed riding. A tailwind and an approaching thunderstorm caused us to increase our pace until we were 16 miles out of town. We stayed at an abandoned farmhouse, with permission. There was much thunder and lightning but little rain. Iowa had rolling hills, and it was never as monotonous as the terrain in southern Kentucky. We had traveled 1400 miles since leaving Cherry Grove, and were a long distance from territory familiar to us. *Moulton, IA, to 16 miles past Mount Ayr, IA, 104 miles.*

May 27: Across the Wide Missouri

On May 27, we arose early to cool and overcast weather. Biking was much more pleasant than what we had experienced on most days before Iowa. We rode into Bedford for breakfast, then Clarinda, Shenandoah, and Sidney where we ate lunch. We had two steep hills to climb before Sidney. When we stopped at Waubonsie State Park for a long rest and shower, we enjoyed the beautiful panorama of an 8-mile-wide plain stretching to the Missouri River.

The plain started the transition from hill to flat country which made us think the biking would be easy for quite a while (wrong!). We crossed the Missouri River into Nebraska at Nebraska City, where we had dinner. The city was the home of John Arbor, founder of Arbor Day, and also on the route followed by Lewis and Clark as they moved up the Missouri River. It rained while we ate, so we waited until the rain decreased and called our families to inform them of our progress. We rode 18 miles in the light rain with water and dirt spraying onto us from our tires. It got dark before we reached our planned destination. Upon seeing a highway patrolman at dusk, we stopped at an abandoned house. The muddy driveway caused our tires to become so encased in mud that they would not turn. I had developed a viral cold and a hacking cough, which lasted for 5-10 minutes every time we stopped biking, but luckily not while riding. *10 miles east of Bedford, IA, to 3 miles west of Syracuse, NE, 105.3 miles.*

THE TRIO'S DAY 16:

May 28: Stig Was Here

On May 28, Sunday, we awoke to the task of removing the mud from our bikes. We had to travel almost 30 miles before we found a restaurant in Lincoln that was open early on a Sunday on Memorial Day weekend. We turned south toward Crete, NE, and rode in the rain. We went to the campus of Doane College (now University) and found it closed. The campus and the surrounding town were beautiful and well worth going out of our way to see. Dan and John Jones were my high school friends who went to Doane. John had graduated a couple years earlier, and Dan had graduated just weeks before and was no longer living there, so we didn't have anyone to connect with. We ate lunch but Vaughn had stomach pains and couldn't eat anything.

By chance we met a policeman as we were leaving Crete, who reported that Stig had been through town early that morning and had left us a message on a post card at the post office, which I still have. Stig had made a super effort to catch us but, apparently, had passed us. We were shocked to learn that Stig was alone, but still biking. We decided to pick up our pace and try to catch him, but the driving rain was a major impediment to chasing Stig immediately. We decided to delay leaving Crete.

> Postcard from Stig intended for the Trio left at post office in Crete NE. Stig had no idea where the Trio was but in fact they were only a few hours behind.

We accepted the policeman's offer to get out of the driving rain and rest in the town jail. We were frisked, had to surrender our belts, and had to sign an agreement. We were locked up from 1:30 to 4:30 PM and slept on our first bed in 14 days. We left town at

5 PM and arrived at York at 8:40 PM. Along the way, Bill took a serious spill when he ran into my back tire.

Stig was not in any obvious location in York, and no one we talked to, including the police, had seen him, or heard about him. We didn't know if he had taken another route or just slipped through town without being noticed by the police. We asked about sleeping in jail but did not qualify because we had more than $4.00. We were clearly too rich for York's jail, but if we had had less cash, we might have been jailed for vagrancy. We ate a late supper and finished riding near 10:00 PM. We slept in a livestock barn at the fairgrounds because we expected it to rain and needed overhead coverage, given that we could see lightning in the distance. After Crete, the land in Nebraska for some time was extremely flat and covered by large farms. *Syracuse, NE, to York, NE, 107.3 miles.*

Sharing the (Wind)Load

Traveling in close single file really reduces wind resistance, as stated previously, for all but the leader. The closer one can follow, the less drag there is. However, following too close increases the risk of running into the

back wheel of the bike in front. When this
happens, the biker behind almost always
has a spill because the biker cannot turn
his wheel in the direction opposite the
contact as a means of regaining control
of the bike. Instead, the front wheel
of the bike turns rapidly in the same
direction as the initial contact without
any chance for correction. The front
biker whose rear wheel is hit usually is
quite stable and this biker doesn't fall.

Bill and Vaughn were frequently the lead bikers
when I had my knee problem early in the trip. This
reduced the stress and pain on my knee. After my
knee improved, sharing the lead was necessary to keep
everyone fresh so that we could bike long distances.
It became very apparent that if one biker faltered, we
all faltered.

THE TRIO'S DAY 17:

May 29: Into the Wind

On May 29, Memorial Day, we slept in (past 6 AM)
and ate breakfast at a restaurant north of York, NE.

We were determined to catch up with Stig, but the wind had other plans for us. The wind was from the northwest 15-20 mph, so we struggled all day long, riding behind each other in a straight line. It was also becoming cold, which marked the transition from hot to relatively cool weather for the rest of the trip. Cool weather made us much more efficient and happier, despite the wind.

We finally covered 48 miles to Grand Island for lunch at 12:30. Vaughn got a flat tire as we were leaving and had to return to town to put air in the tire (our pumps were lightweight, fragile, and no longer functional). We rode to Gibbon and, following the advice of a young policeman, stayed at Windmill State Recreational Area. Again, the police had seen nothing of Stig. There was no shelter from the rain, wind, and cold other than the campgrounds, so for the first time we paid a camping fee of $2.50 and slept inside the toilet house under the sinks. Luckily, only one camper had to use the urinal before we moved out, and he had good aim. We didn't cover much ground this day because of the late start, terrible headwind, and rain. *York, NE, to Windmill Recreational Area, NE, 79.6 miles.*

THE TRIO'S DAY 18:

May 30: Riding Out the Wind

On May 30, we arose early, took a shower, and biked to Kearney for breakfast, and to buy new tires for Bill and Vaughn. Somehow, I never had a flat or changed my tires on the entire trip. I did switch tire positions (rotated) from front to back once (May 31). My bike had touring tires which were thicker and heavier than the lightweight tires of Bill and Vaughn, which were standard on their racing bicycles.

We kept imagining that Stig must be just ahead of us but that we couldn't catch him because of our slow progress. Yet, no one reported seeing him when we asked at towns and restaurants along the way. We headed west on US 30, following the Union Pacific Railroad track while fighting the wind. Silos for storing alfalfa, which was being dried on giant heated rolling drums, could be seen from five miles away because of the flat land. We used these silos to provide interim goals for the difficult progress. The wind drag made us suffer. We would have gladly traded the flat land for hills if we could have stopped the wind. We couldn't talk, and the land was monotonous. Each biker dreaded his turn to take the lead and break the wind. Despite the great effort, progress was slow.

We ate lunch at Cozad, NE, around 3:30 PM because the wind caused such slow progress. The wind died down after Cozad, on the way to North Platte. We started to parallel the Nebraska sandhills later in the day and continued to parallel the railroad. With about nine miles to go before North Platte, Vaughn had a flat tire. We had no functioning pump to inflate the tire, so Vaughn had to hitchhike to North Platte. Bill and I did a sprint to beat darkness, crossing the North Platte River before finding Vaughn with his bike ready to go.

 Vaughn discovered that he had a broken axle but elected to ignore it until some future time. Luckily, his bike had quick release hubs, which use a lever to progressively snug the wheel hub to the bike frame without the need for bolting the axle. Quick release hubs do, however, depend on a transaxle rod that could also break and leave the wheel without any attachment and cause a catastrophic failure at high speeds.

We ate supper, and at 11 PM, slept in a city park with the permission of police. Despite our concerns early on, throughout the entire trip, police were extremely helpful and never impeded our progress or harassed us. We repeatedly asked police if they had seen a lone bicyclist or heard of Stig, but after Crete, NE, no one could remember hearing about or seeing Stig for many miles and days. *Windmill State Recreational Area to North Platte, NE, 116.6 miles.*

THE TRIO'S DAY 19:

May 31: A Great Day

On May 31, we had breakfast near the city park. The morning temperature was 49 degrees. We began riding about 8 AM and crossed into the Mountain Time Zone, gaining an hour. We were flanked by the sandhills to the north and the South Platte River to the south. We had lunch in Ogallala, which first gained fame as the terminus for cattle drives that traveled from Texas to the Union Pacific railhead. We then left by US 26 north toward Lake McConaughy.

The scenery and riding were spectacular. We had the road nearly to ourselves and for 30 miles we saw no towns. When we first saw Lake McConaughy, we were high above the lake. Many interesting, eroded canyons led down to the reservoir. Near the western end of the lake was Ash Hollow State Historical Park, where the

Mormons had crossed the North Platte River by use of block and tackle equipment and branched off from the Oregon Trail in their own journey West. Ruts etched into the road by the wagons are still visible on the bluffs. We then rode into Lewellen, NE where Bill had his second flat tire of the trip. We had an ice cream snack and then proceeded to Oshkosh for dinner at 6:30. Eager to keep moving, we then continued westward for eight miles more and camped in a pasture that we determined was bull-free. It was a great day, probably the best up to that point. We were already at 3,400 feet in altitude, yet we seemed to climb effortlessly. *North Platte, NE, to 8 miles west of Oshkosh, NE, 103.6 miles.*

THE TRIO'S DAY 20:

June 1: Chimney Rock

On June 1, we woke up to see deer close by in the pasture. We ate breakfast in Lisco, NE, where we met a Hamms beer truck driver who was very interested in our trip. We had a long discussion about our experiences and about what we could expect on the road ahead. We continued across the North Platte River at Bridgeport. Vaughn had yet another flat which he repaired at Northport. We saw increasing wildlife: hares, hawks, deer, and even a coyote.

We arrived at Chimney Rock National Monument, a landmark for pioneers heading west. The day was warm with the temperature at 90 degrees, but it was not humid. This made riding much more comfortable than we had been experiencing for most of the trip. We covered 70 miles before stopping for lunch in Gering. We visited the North Platte Valley Museum.

As we were leaving Gering, we ran into the Hamms beer man from breakfast. He was obviously making the rounds. We continued to the Scotts Bluff National Monument. The Scotts Bluff Museum had the largest collection of paintings by the western painter William Henry Jackson (not to be confused with Bill Jackson). Bill and I hitched a ride to the top of the monument (800 feet) with a park ranger, while Vaughn walked. There was a great panoramic view in all directions. We returned to our bikes by walking down the monument road.

For settlers heading west, Chimney Rock was by far the most frequently mentioned landmark. It can be seen long before travelers arrive at its base. A slender spire rises 325 feet above its base. Volcanic ash and clay were eroded

from nearby bluffs to create the spire.
Chimney Rock and its surrounding area
look today much the way they did when
the first European settlers passed
through in the mid-1800s. It can also be
seen from the top of Scotts Bluff, which
is about 23 miles farther northwest. We
were excited to reach these important
landmarks just like the western settlers
before us.

We left for Torrington, WY, at 5:30 PM and
covered the 33 miles by 7:30 PM, which was a torrid
pace for us (even if it isn't for the *Tour de France*).
This stretch showed how much our conditioning
had improved. We ate dinner in Torrington and
again spent the night voluntarily in jail. The police
lieutenant and radio operator were among the
friendliest people we met on the trip. Once again,
we had to surrender our valuables and belts (so we
couldn't hang ourselves) but we could use pens to
write our postcards. Of note, we did not spend time
in the Wyoming Medium Correctional Institution,
also in Torrington. Our entry into Wyoming was
exciting because it heralded the beginning of our
experiences with the Rocky Mountains. *Oshkosh, NE,
to Torrington, WY, 107 miles.*

THE TRIO'S DAY 21:

June 2: First Sighting
of the Rockies

On June 2, Friday, we were released from jail at 5:30 AM per our request. Our fingerprints had to be taken in triplicate as a price to pay for staying in jail, one copy each to the local police, state police, and FBI. We ate breakfast and then asked the Wyoming Port of Entry about permission to travel on Interstate 25, which was about the only reasonable way from Torrington to Douglas, Wyoming. We were told we would probably not be harassed by the highway patrol, especially since there were only 21 officers for the entire state.

 We passed through Fort Laramie, which once was the best-known military post and mail route on the northern plains before it was abandoned in 1890. The fort witnessed the saga of America's westward expansion and the Native American resistance to encroachment on their territories.

We gradually climbed on I-25 to Glendo where we ate lunch. After lunch we went to the Glendo Reservoir for a quick dip in the cold water, which was always refreshing. We then had to duck under a bridge to escape thunderstorms. Again, we crossed the North Platte River near Orin, and arrived in Douglas, after a long downhill coast, for dinner. The scenery had been magnificent. We then did our laundry and wrote home.

During the day we saw Laramie Peak at 10,274 feet elevation, our first sighting of the Rockies. The Laramie Mountains were named after the French trapper LaRamie, who disappeared into the mountains in the late 1810s. We saw dead rattlesnakes on the road, observed a cowboy herding cattle (just like on TV), and spent the night in a camping area, moving under a camping trailer when it started to rain. We were not sure whether the trailer was occupied but decided to quietly sleep underneath without waking any occupants to ask permission. Such a move always risked waking up at gunpoint, but we planned to get moving very early in the morning. *Torrington, WY, to Douglas, WY, 99.8 miles.*

THE TRIO'S DAY 22:

June 3: The Old West

On June 3, we awoke with our sleeping bags almost dry despite a vicious thunderstorm overnight. We ate breakfast in Douglas, WY, at the same restaurant where we had eaten dinner the previous night and resumed cycling on I-25 for 28 straight miles without a rest. The road and outside temperature were ideal, and the view was scenic.

I felt we were in the old West that is pictured in so many movies. If we had been chased by western outlaws on horses, the horse could have easily outrun our bicycles because a galloping horse can exceed 50 mph. Only a professional bicycle athlete can maintain over 25 mph on flat ground for prolonged periods. However, a human traveling 15 mph on a bicycle is the most energy efficient means of human transportation, even more efficient than travel by horse.[iv]

At Glenrock we saw, maybe, 50 antelope, along with many oil wells. We ate lunch at McDonalds in East Casper, our only visit to the "Golden Arches" of the journey. We located a bicycle shop, hoping to repair Vaughn's broken rear axle before some serious accident happened. Unfortunately, this repair didn't happen. Vaughn was able to get a new tire and some mail he had prearranged for East Casper. We left town at 2 PM and passed through dull landscape until we reached Hell's Half Acre, where we ate dinner at an expensive restaurant, because it was the only option.

We ordered from the breakfast menu because those options were the least expensive. It rained hard while we were there which delayed our trip for two hours. We rode to Hiland, where the owner of a closed hotel opened up a room for us. Among the interesting landmarks we saw along the road were Poison Creek, Poisonous Spider Creek, and the Rattlesnake Mountain Range. *Douglas, WY, to Hiland, WY, 111.2 miles.*

Hell's Half Acre is really a misnomer since there are over 900 acres of spectacular rock formations. At one time it was used by the Indians as a buffalo hunting trap. Indian legend suggested that it emitted flames and gaseous fumes, and this may be the origin of the satanic reference to Hell' in its name. We were amazed by the canyons and the broad panorama of natural sculptures.

THE TRIO'S DAY 23:

June 4: The Wild West

On June 4, Sunday, we arose to a beautiful day and biked 20 miles to breakfast at a grocery store in Moneta, WY, where we had oven-warmed sandwiches. We got word that Stig had passed through two days before alone, confirming his moxie and accelerated pace compared to ours. We hadn't been able to catch up with him, but we were determined to try. We felt that he was also headed toward Jackson, Wyoming, as planned, and that we might meet in this small town, or at least get an exact determination about how far ahead of us he was.

As long as we knew Stig was still biking, we were determined in our quest to reunite. Vaughn and I had milkshakes in Shoshoni; it seemed that we could eat all the ice cream we wanted with no worry about getting fat. We saw occasional herds of sheep near Thermopolis, WY, which was 30 miles away and named for a city in Greece. Greeks used sheep for transportation in their ancient literature, which was ingenious, but not nearly as efficient, safe, or disciplined as travel by bicycle is now. But each has its place in the history and lore of mankind.

We decided to keep an eye out for more sheep. We biked through desolate country until noon when we could see the snowcapped mountains of the Wind River Range, which was exciting. We continued to climb for the remainder of the day heading toward Dubois. We took shortcuts and rode on dirt and sand for seven miles. This was our first travel on a dirt road. It was so devoid of signage that we were lucky we took the correct turns to return to the main highway. The bicycles swayed clumsily as we biked in the unstable sand. We saw a reservoir and intricate irrigation systems, but the area was dry and dusty.

Even the highways were barren of gas stations, stores, and restaurants. We always carried enough water with us and never ran out during the entire trip. Our water needs were markedly increased from before we reached the mountains because of the high altitude, and low humidity. We finally came upon a store and cafe after crossing the Wind River, where we had lunch (quick warmed hamburgers) after biking 89 miles. We rested and talked to the proprietor for two and a half hours. He told stories that embellished our view of the West. We then rode to Crowheart Butte near Burris, which had some fascinating geological formations.

The battle of Crowheart Butte in 1866 is one of the most interesting in local Indian folklore. The Butte was the site of a fierce battle between the Shoshone and Crow Indian tribes. After five days of fighting on or near the Butte there was a stalemate. In order to save lives, the Shoshone Chief Washakie approached the Crow Chief Big Robber with a proposal for single chief-against-chief combat to death, with the losers tribe leaving the disputed Wind River hunting territory. Chief Washakie prevailed and cut out the heart of Big Robber and displayed it on his lance. The Crow Indians left the Wind River territory. The Shoshone had occupied the area for some time. It was the Shoshone tribe that had assisted the Lewis and Clark Expedition 60 years earlier when Sacagawea was united with her native tribe. Members of the Shoshone tribe guided the expedition through the Rocky Mountains and on to the Columbia River. The tribe also traded horses to the explorers for guns and other goods.

We stopped at a cafe along the highway, looking for refreshments, but found it closed and encountered two men who appeared drunk. These characters began shooting a pistol just to scare us. They succeeded. We sensed developing danger, although it seemed very unlikely that the bullets would land on anyone by chance in remote Wyoming. We just didn't want any bullets to land directly on us, on purpose or by accident.

I was worried the gunmen were dangerous criminals hiding out in the closed cafe. We made no attempt to report the men, or any others that were aggressive to us, to authorities, because the men could retaliate very easily given that we were so vulnerable. It was encounters like this one that worried us about Stig traveling alone, although we felt he could handle just about any situation since he had apparently traveled alone from Hannibal to Wyoming.

We continued to Dubois, following the beautiful Wind River, and arrived at 7:30 just in time to see the remnants of a rodeo and some wild cowboys. Rodeos seemed to be a popular form of recreation for Wyoming because we saw many leaflets advertising upcoming rodeos. Dubois is at 6917 feet, 2000 feet above the day's low point. Climbing was no longer a problem for us, and we set a distance record despite the climbs that day. We ate dinner and then got permission to spend the night in the basement of Our Lady of the Woods Catholic Church. Bill and I were of the Catholic faith but were unable to attend Mass during the trip due to scheduling, timing, and scarcity of churches along our route. We expected a cold and rainy night and welcomed the shelter. *Hiland, WY, to Dubois, WY, 134.2 miles.*

CHAPTER SEVEN

STIG TELLS HIS STORY – HE CAN DO IT ALONE

STIG

STIG'S DAY 16:

May 28: Storms on the Plains

On the morning of May 28th, I left Crete on N-33 feeling blessed with the fullness of experiences from the previous days and wondered what new adventures might unfold. My mood soon shifted as the clouds overhead darkened, signaling imminent rain. I found it ironic that rain started to fall heavily in the small town called Friend, 18 miles west of Crete. I pulled into the town's only gas station for shelter and to wait for the storm to abate. While taking a pause here, the gas station attendant told me tornado warnings were in effect.

After several hours, the rain stopped, and I headed west toward Hastings. During this next stretch the terrain was flat and boring for perhaps 20 miles. Then heavy rain and wind resumed, more intense than before. I became overridden with anxiety. I periodically faced 20-30 mph headwinds with short gusts probably up to 50 mph. While this was not a tornado, the conditions were severe. Large trucks frequently passed me, sometimes blowing me off the road almost into the parallel ditch. It was difficult to stand, let alone bicycle in traffic. I felt terrified and further aggravated by my continuous need to wipe water droplets from my glasses.

I sorely missed my cycling friends, especially the teamwork for breaking headwinds, and our discussions for how to confront challenges. The slow, torturous, and interrupted cycling broke my spirit and, about 30 miles west of Friend, I stopped on the roadside to try to hitch a ride out of the miserable weather. After standing on the roadside shivering and drenched for an interminable time, I was able to get a ride north to Litchfield, and shortly thereafter, still in the rain, another ride to just short of Ainsworth, NE. During this ride I sorely missed my bicycling buddies. Since there had been no messages from them at the post office in Crete, I imagined they were probably behind me that morning. I didn't think they would have dropped out since they were so committed and so much effort had gone into their planning. I wanted to be with the group again but now saw those chances ebbing.

I cycled into Ainsworth late in the afternoon under patches of blue sky and sunshine. I felt somewhat guilty for breaking from the continuous sequence of cycling by catching rides. I realized I could have minimized the cycling break by just hitching to the nearest town and waiting the storm out before resuming. However, when given that opportunity, I had chosen to go for as long as the ride would take me, and then for another one after that.

I saw these choices as being character weakness in myself that I had experienced before, and that I no doubt would be challenged with again. I thought again of my three biking friends and wondered where they might be and if, in the same conditions, what they might be doing. I longed for the resilience and support that I had felt when riding with my friends and questioned the decision I had made back near Hannibal of not rejoining them when given that opportunity. Now that I had hitched rides north for probably a few hundred miles, the prospects of meeting up with my friends seemed dimmer than ever.

A Memorable Evening

In Ainsworth I sought the county jail for a place to stay. Here I met the most unforgettable character of the entire trip, Rusty Davis. He was the county sheriff, a towering, heavy-set, muscular man in his 60's with a huge graying mustache, giant leather cowboy hat, and voice that spoke from his belly. His mere presence conveyed a life lived fully. Rusty said that I could sleep in one of the two empty jail cells if I was willing to be searched and locked up for the night. I gratefully agreed. Much to my delight, he invited me to join him for dinner in his house adjacent to the county jail, appearing as curious about my journey as I was of his.

Rusty told me he had been ranked 10th in line to be the Heavyweight Champion of the world in the early 1930's when Joe Louis was beginning his reign. He then went on to become a professional rodeo rider, joined the Navy to see the world (including playing football for them), married a woman in Honolulu, came back to Nebraska after World War Two to buy a cattle ranch, lost everything in the Blizzard of 1949, and started over running a post office, until more recently becoming a sheriff. As I heard his story, I thought of Henry David Thoreau's words from Walden Pond: "I went to the woods because I wished to live deliberately, to front only the essential facts of life, and see if I could not learn what it had to teach, and not, when I came to die, discover that I had not lived."

This aspiration for living fully, and the life of Rusty, would inspire me for many years. *Crete, NE, to Ainsworth, NE, 50 miles by bicycle, ~ 200 miles by hitching.*

STIG'S DAY 17:

May 29: A Welcome Day Off

On May 29th, Rusty suggested I stay another day so that he could show me the countryside. I gratefully obliged. I also used this off-day to replace three spokes and true both of my wheels, as they had started to wobble. Rusty drove me around in his pickup truck and told me about the terrain and the great underground lake beneath much of Nebraska (also known as the Ogallala Aquifer). I learned about Herefords, Angus, Holsteins, and Charolais cattle, and that it takes 1 to 15 acres of land per head to raise them, depending on the nature of the soil. I also learned that it takes about 90 pounds of grass, or seven pounds of corn, to yield one pound of meat, and that some cows can yield as much as 20 gallons of milk per day. I saw hundreds of different cows and bulls that day and felt such a close affinity with these gentle creatures that I stopped eating beef, unless served as a guest, from that day forward. *No bicycle mileage.*

STIG S DAY 18:

May 30: A Giant Ball of String

On May 30th I left with a full breakfast and a warm send off from Rusty, heading west on US 20. The terrain was mostly flat, offering small intermittent towns generally spaced 10-20 miles apart, making stops convenient for short breaks along the way. During one of these stops I came upon a grocery store that had the biggest roadside curiosity of the day — a giant ball of string, maybe five feet in diameter, that was 45 miles long. While this was the largest ball of string that I had ever seen, it was not much of a curiosity for most of the visitors passing through. I learned that this might be because a few hundred miles southeast of this location, in Cawker City, KS, resided a ball of sisal twine of more than 10 feet in diameter, reputedly one of the largest in the world. More importantly for me, for most of the day, there was little wind and no rain. The verdant green scenery approaching Gordon provided the most memorable moment of the day, a spectacular contrast to the previous mostly brownish terrain. *Ainsworth, NE, to Gordon NE, 137 miles.*

STIG'S DAY 19:

May 31: A Memorable Milkshake

On May 31st I continued on route US 20 between Gordon and Harrison following along the Fremont, Elkhorn, and Missouri Valley Railroad that had been completed from Omaha, Nebraska to Wyoming in the 1880's. This region is in the northern Sandhills of Nebraska which native American Indians had populated for thousands of years before the white man came. I found Chadron, NE, the first major town I came to after 47 miles, to be particularly striking given its heavy green vegetation in contrast to the peripheral brown terrain.

The other memorable waypoint of the day came in Crawford, NE, and the nearby Fort Robinson State Park (24 miles west of Chadron), which provided another striking contrast of green within versus brown surrounding terrain.

By contrast, my main entertainment in Crawford was a chocolate milkshake at the grocery store in the middle of town. That held me over until Harrison, 27 miles further west on US 20. There, I met a man named John Herren in the public park, who invited me to stay in his home for the night where I showered, shaved, dined, and shared stories of my journey with him and his wife. *Gordon, NE, to Harrison, NE, 98 miles.*

The war chief Crazy Horse, renown for leading several tribes to victory at Little Big Horn (also known as Custer's Last Stand), had surrendered with his defenders in 1877 at Fort Robinson. In the 1880s Crawford was a wild frontier town, with saloons, brothels, and dancing girls brought in by Calamity Jane, all of which purportedly catered to the soldiers in Fort Robinson.

STIG'S DAY 20:

June 1: The Rockies in View

On June 1, with a generous lunch pack to go from the Herren's, I continued west on US20, excited about the prospect of soon crossing into Wyoming. After confronting strong headwinds for about 30 miles, an old man slowly drove up in his pick-up truck adjacent to where I was riding and offered me a lift. The headwinds had been an absolute grind and I could not resist. I got a ride for about 30 miles to Lost Springs, a desolate area that had gotten its name in the 1880's from railroad workers who could not find the springs shown on survey maps of the area. At Lost Springs, the wind was still howling and, just as I was about to resume cycling, an American Indian in an old school bus offered me a lift to Douglas for another 20 miles. Not wanting to confront the wind, I gratefully accepted and sat next to the driver. He passionately spoke about his boxing career, his hands periodically leaving the steering wheel in wild gesticulation. I imagined the bus swerving into the roadside ditch, my life ending prematurely. I reflected again on my weakness of character for accepting the ride but rationalized that I had still made a wise choice.

In Douglas, I got my first glimpse of the Rockies. The vista offered by the vast open terrain highlighted by the distant white cap of Mt. Laramie was spectacular. I resumed cycling toward Casper and, now with no headwind and easy heart, made great time. I found a large bike shop in Casper and had both my wheels realigned. The mechanic told me that a couple on a 10-speed tandem and a family of five had recently passed through en route to St Louis. He mentioned that every year about 50 people pass through, bicycling across country, mostly from west to east to get assistance from the prevailing westerlies. I also somewhat regretted that I was not doing the west to east path across the States. At the bike shop I met the Dalton family who invited me to overnight in their home. It was a lively evening as they had six kids — all interested in hearing about my travel adventures. *Harrison, NE, to Casper, WY. 88 miles of cycling, 50 miles of lift.*

STIG'S DAY 21:

June 2: Changing Views

On June 2nd, with a huge lunch pack provided by the Daltons, I continued west on US20 toward Riverton. I especially appreciated their provisions as the distances between towns were becoming longer and longer. The wind-worn rocks and snowcaps in the Rockies, as seen from the city of Shoshoni, marked the highlight of the day's journey. In Riverton, so named because of it being at the confluence of the Big and Wind Rivers, I stayed at the minister's house near their Presbyterian church. He and his wife, now with six children, had worked as missionaries in Asia. After a warm shower I joined them for a lively family dinner. *Casper, WY, to Riverton, WY, 122 miles.*

STIG'S DAY 22:

June 3: Sleeping in Church

On June 3rd I set forth for Dubois, continuing on US20. After leaving Riverton, WY, the scenery became barren and uninteresting for much of the way, except for stretches that would come close to, or cross, Wind River. I could hardly feel the mostly gradual climb in elevation, and as I got closer to Dubois, I became excited about the prospect of soon crossing the Rockies. I arrived in Dubois near sunset and considered seeking refuge for the night in one of their churches. When I came upon the St. Thomas Episcopal Church of Dubois this seemed perfect, as I had been in the choir and served as an acolyte in St. Mark's Episcopal Church in Jackson Heights, New York City from age 8-14.

Even though I had a painful memory of being told by the choir master to pipe down with my exuberant singing because I was a bit off key, I had many happy memories of bonding with friends and youth leaders at St. Marks. As I got older in high school, my refuge on Sundays became, more and more, playing golf on the public golf courses of New York City than being at St. Marks. I couldn't partake in both during the same Sunday because playing golf on the public courses was an all-day affair — taking the bus and/or subway to the course, then waiting 3-5 hours before being able to play, then being forced to play slowly because of waiting time on each hole, then returning home again by public transportation.

I found the priest at St. Thomas, told him my story, and he invited me to sleep in one of the pews if I ensured that I would be gone before the beginning of the Sunday 10 AM service. He told me that their church had been founded by an Episcopal missionary in 1910 who served the Native American tribes on the Wind River. Grateful for the accommodation, I quickly settled into one of the pews in the back of the church, and after waiting for about 1/2 hour, hoping that nobody would catch me in the act, quickly devoured two peanut butter and jelly sandwiches that I had carried from Riverton. I could smell the leftover odor of the peanut butter and worried about the extent to which this might linger come morning. I went to sleep trusting that I would awaken and be gone before any early Sunday morning arrivals. *Riverton, WY, to Dubois, WY, 91 miles.*

STIGS DAY 23:

June 4: From Here You Can Go Anywhere

On June 4th, much to my surprise I woke up in the morning hearing the organ and voices of the choir of St. Thomas Episcopal Church. I pondered my dilemma, and gingerly lifted my head over the pew, hoping not to be seen, and discovered with great relief that it was just a practice before the service. I quickly pulled my belongings together, stealthily exited the church, and headed northwest on US 26 toward Togwotee Pass.

I found the gradual climb from Dubois (6946 ft) to Togwotee Pass (9658 ft), covering 33 miles, to be breathtaking and filled with excitement in anticipation of crossing a continental divide for the first time in my life. Doing this by bicycle and knowing that a hard-earned reward of downhill lay on the other side of the pass, filled my body with adrenaline. "Togwotee" means "lance thrower" or "exactly there," from an Indian lance-throwing game. It has also been translated to mean "from here you can go anywhere" — a sense that I was beginning to have more and more as the journey continued.

When I got to the top of the pass, I stopped to throw a few snowballs at different pine trees. The descent was even more spectacular than the climb. The distant mighty Tetons looked like giant teepees in their triangular geometry and purple blue like colors. During the downward coast I accelerated rapidly, probably reaching speeds of 50 miles per hour. However, I was soon overcome by fear and gradually applied the brakes, afraid of braking too quickly and being cast forward and having a serious accident, especially not wearing a helmet. The cold windchill during the descent also tempered my excitement, but this soon dissipated as I reached lower elevation and coasted at lower speeds in flatter terrain.

The day was filled with scenic stops continuing along US26 and then on US89N, through various ups and downs, en route to Grand Loop Road, and finally to Old Faithful. I arrived in the Old Faithful Historic District in the evening, in time for one of its eruptions before sunset. When I told the concierge at the Old Faithful Lodge about my low budget bicycle trip across the US, he offered me free floor space in one of their storage rooms, where I slept for the night. *Dubois, WY, to Old Faithful, WY, 122 miles.*

STIG'S DAY 24:

June 5: Old Friends

On the morning of June 5th after doing another walk around Old Faithful and the surrounding geysers, I returned to Old Faithful Lodge for breakfast and to pick up some sandwiches for the road. I then cycled north, experiencing more fantastic scenery on Grand Loop Road for 16 miles before turning left onto Entrance Road and then 14 miles further onto Yellowstone Avenue. Crossing into Montana was another milestone westward, the beginning of the 10th state to bicycle through.

When I pulled up to the Eagle Store in West Yellowstone before noon another unusual event occurred. Given that West Yellowstone is a small town (then about 700 year-round residents), I had planned to try and track down Pete and Verlee Zupan, some old friends that I had been out of touch with for several years. I knew they had retired to live here but did not know their address. When I pulled up to the entrance of the Eagle Store, I saw a gentleman who I thought was Pete exiting the store with some supplies in his hands.

Immediately thereafter, as he looked up approaching a pick-up truck, he saw me, and we stared at each other both aghast — he was bellowing out "Stig" and I bellowed out "Pete". After a big bear hug, and exclamations of equal wonderment, he invited me home. I spent the day and night with Pete and Verlee, sharing my bicycle adventures and reminiscing about the summers of 1967 and 1968 when we had all worked at Elizabeth Arden's beauty spa, Maine Chance Farm, in the Belgrade Lake region of Maine. Pete and I had been chauffeurs, transporting elite clients to and from either the Augusta or Portland airport and the spa, and from their on-site residences to the various spa facilities. Verlee had been a masseuse. We lived on the Maine Chance Farm property in adjacent rooms of a small wooden house, and ate at a common dining facility for breakfast, lunch, and dinner, as did 15-20 other on-site staff. Pete and Verlee had worked for Elizabeth Arden for many summers at Maine Chance Farm, as well as at the winter spa in Scottsdale AZ.

I had grown very close to Pete and Verlee during those summers, and when they asked me to stay for a few more days it was heart wrenching to decline, but I knew I had to keep moving. *Old Faithful Lodge, WY, to West Yellowstone, MT, 32 miles.*

STIGS DAY 25:

June 6: Gold Country

I woke up in the home of Pete and Verlee on June 6th and the temperature outside was below freezing. This is not uncommon for West Yellowstone, which has a monthly low June average temperature a few degrees above freezing. The town's December monthly record low of -59 °F (-51 °C) is the lowest of the lower 48 states. After a full breakfast, I departed with tearful eyes of gratitude, not only for this short stay, but for all that Pete and Verlee had done for me when I was a newbie working for Elizabeth Arden in Maine.

I found the scenery, northwest-bound out of West Yellowstone, with blue lakes contrasted with background snow-capped mountains to be breathtaking. The ride NW on US287, often parallel to and sometimes crossing the Madison River, was mostly flat and refreshing. The river converges with the Jefferson and Gallatin rivers at Three Forks, MT, to form the Missouri River, about 80 miles north of where I was. Madison River was named by Meriwether

Lewis after James Madison, then Secretary of State under Thomas Jefferson, during the Lewis and Clark expeditions in 1805.

A stretch between Ennis and Virginia City presented a steep climb similar in duration to the climb into Boone, TN, but now being in much better shape, I actually enjoyed this.

I rolled into Virginia City near dusk, delighted by its striking preserved history. Once in town, I quickly learned that when prospectors discovered gold near Alder Creek in 1863, a gold rush began and so Ennis, and more notably Virginia City, became boom towns supporting fortune seekers. In Virginia City I had a sense of being transported back to the gold rush time due to authentically restored historic buildings. This visual impression became further reinforced when I was invited by the owner to spend the night alone in his candle store on Main Street. *West Yellowstone, MT, to Virginia City, MT, 88 miles.*

STIG'S DAY 26:

June 7: Racing the Rain

On June 7th I woke to a nauseating smell of candles hanging on strings across the room below the ceiling. I think I was too tired the night before to be bothered by this smell. After a giant milkshake for breakfast at the candle store, I rode 72 miles to Butte, MT with only brief rest stops, aided by a tailwind and fueled further by a banana, a Milky Way, and two Baby Ruth bars. The highlight of this stretch occurred about halfway toward Butte when I approached two large herds of cattle steered by shouting cowboys with active whips down the road in front of me. I hesitated trying forward passage through the herd out of fear of being crushed, but encouraged by one of the cowboys, I decided to try and cycle through them. Sure enough, the cattle parted to let me through, and I momentarily imagined feeling like Moses parting the Red Sea before continuing on to Butte.

I did not find Butte particularly interesting, except that when I stopped in a grocery store for food supplies, the owner gave me an assortment of fruit in exchange for me delivering a message to a relative in Portland, OR. West of Butte, prior to Deer Lodge, on I 90W I encountered many large moving trucks and heavy clouds of dust being kicked up from the road, often making breathing difficult. In Deer Lodge, I met another cyclist who bought me a beer.

I showered for $0.80 at a KOA campground before cycling very fast for the last 15 miles of the day to beat out a rainstorm, accompanied by lightning, that was approaching from the rear. This was a very unusual situation where my bicycle speed was the same as the approaching rain falling on the roadside about 200 feet behind me. When I peeked behind over my shoulder, I could see the color of the darkening road moving at the same speed as my bicycle. I experimented with this eerie predicament, periodically slowing a little bit to hear the rain getting closer and then, speeding up to hear the rain receding. I entered Drummond with great relief and was allowed to sleep in St. Michael's Catholic Church for the night. *Virginia City, MT, to Drummond, MT, 144 miles.*

STIG'S DAY 27:

June 8: Hot Spring, Cold Night

On June 8th, after having a $1 breakfast of hotcakes in a Drummond diner, I set forth on Route 12 W. I enjoyed the gradual downhill to Missoula following along Clark Fork, a tributary of the Clark River (so named after the explorer in the Lewis and Clark Expedition). The highlight of the day occurred during the 2000 foot climb up from Missoula to Lolo Pass (5200 feet elevation at the border between Montana and Idaho), a break for a swim in the hot spring near the Lolo Pass visitor center, and then a downward descent of about 1500 feet for 20 miles through the

Idaho National Forest to the Powell Campground just off the roadside.

The gushing of white water and nearby fir, spruce, and cedar trees alongside most of the curving Route 12 presented quite an adventure. In the Powell Campground I found a campsite adjacent to a retired miner and his camp trailer and built a campfire. We talked into the night about our travels. Initially he had found his itinerant lifestyle exciting in seeing so many new places, but now, after several years of this, he had grown weary. He wanted to settle down somewhere but was not yet sure where that might be. I eventually retired into my sleeping bag perched on top of a wooden bench, reflecting upon the miles covered that day, and quickly fell asleep. I awoke in the middle of the night, freezing and feeling very uncomfortable, but lacking any more clothing to help persevere until morning. *Drummond, MT, to Powell Campground in Idaho National Forest via Lolo Pass. 114 miles.*

CHAPTER EIGHT

THE TRIO CLIMBS THE ROCKY MOUNTAINS AND BEYOND

BRYAN

THE TRIO'S DAY 24:

June 5: Conquering the Pass

On June 5, we got a late start out of Dubois, WY, because it was very cold, and our planned destination was only 55 miles away. However, a mountain pass called Togwotee had to be conquered first. The legends about the impossible climb to Togwotee Pass had been building for a couple of days. We mailed home all unnecessary weight and Bill fixed his bike from an accident I had caused by stopping too quickly. I apologized but Bill was angry for a short time. When one is climbing a steep hill, a biker doesn't have to use the hand brakes to stop rapidly; all he needs to do is stop pedaling. Thus, he must continuously pedal on a hill unless he warns those behind him that he plans to stop. We learned to give verbal warnings if we needed to stop.

We ate breakfast in Dubois and started biking at 9:30 AM, by far our latest start. We climbed all hills that day without problems, and went above the snow line, where we stopped for a snowball fight (what a coincidence, Stig had also had a snowball "fight" one day earlier on the same Pass as we did!). It was very cold, but we generated so much body heat through cycling that we felt comfortable without coats. I was only wearing both my shirts in layers to keep warm.

We followed the Wind River much of the way to the pass which is where the river originates. Vaughn led the way as we crossed the Togwotee Pass and Continental Divide at 9658 feet, the highest elevation of the trip. This was the highlight of the trip because we now felt we could conquer any mountain highway, and thus we were going to succeed in biking cross country. We met some tourists who were surprised that we had ridden our bicycles up through the pass. We stopped at Togwotee Lodge for a snack and to celebrate our success at climbing.

Bryan and Vaughn reaching the highest point of the trip.

No one mentioned Stig to us, even though he had just passed by on this exact route one day earlier. The scenery was gorgeous when we were climbing to the pass and even better when we glided at a high rate of speed (estimated 50 mph) down the other side of the mountain toward the Teton Mountains, which were enormously beautiful especially when we saw them for the first time. On the downward glide, the cold wind blew through our hair and chilled us, especially our faces. We were going so fast that we had to slow down to avoid the car in front of us. Another car followed close behind, forcing us to maintain a very dangerous pace.

Our eyes searched the roadway for potholes or obstacles to avoid colliding with them on our bikes. A collision at high speed would mean instant loss of control and falling to the pavement with a car following close behind, possibly unable to stop before hitting us. But the beauty of the scenery and the dangerous speed were exhilarating, causing us to ignore the reality of what would happen if the car in front of us slowed down quickly, we got a flat tire, or if we hit an obstacle.

The Teton Mountains were a great distraction and caused us to take our eyes off the road and the cars surrounding us. All the days of bland scenery were forgotten. The painful climb to the Togwotee Pass was forgotten. As we rushed down the steep mountain road into the valley, the view of the Teton Mountains was finally obstructed by the trees. Bill tried to stop too fast from his high speed to take a picture and nearly had a major accident. He skidded sideways and lost control of his bike. Only the gyroscopic force of his rapidly turning tires stabilized his bike and prevented disaster.

This high-speed ride down a steep hill from the Togwotee Pass was just one of numerous dangerous thrill rides down mountains without using helmets. We ate at a grocery store near Moran and stayed there at a KOA campground for 2 nights at $3.50 each per night. This was only the second time we had paid to sleep for the night. Hot showers and a grocery store were available, and the manager Sandy Gough loaned

us a tent and, if necessary, the use of his car. We cooked
supper (canned chili) for the first time.

Vaughn with eyeglasses he broke
during the trip with gorgeous Teton
mountains in background.

Our campsite faced the majestic Tetons, about 10-
15 miles away. The scenery was more beautiful than
we had imagined. Other campers and the manager
gathered around us and our bicycles to hear about our
trip. The stories around the campfire were coming
fast and furious, both to and from us. We heard a
story about a man who got out of his camper in his
underwear when his wife, unknowingly, drove off and
had to be stopped by state troopers after 80 miles. I'm

not sure if this story was real or a rural legend. With the help of the camp manager Mr. Gough, we met the Norton family who offered to let us ride in their car through Yellowstone Park the next day. We had fallen into a golden situation which I coined as "fat city." *Dubois, WY, to Moran, WY, 51.5 miles.*

THE TRIO S DAY 25:

June 6: Fat City"

On June 6, we ate at the grocery store and met the Nortons at 8 AM for the car trip into Yellowstone National Park. Mr. and Mrs. Norton had two girls, Terri, and Tammi, and all four sat in the front. This was an inconvenience about which they never complained. As the car arrived at the dual entrance to Yellowstone and Teton Parks, the Nortons would not allow us to pay the $2 entrance fee.

This was the year of the National Parks Centennial. In 1872 Yellowstone National Park was established as the United States' first national park by President Ulysses S Grant, also becoming the world's first national park. Deep snow surrounded the road near the entrance. We traveled the park loop for over 150 miles and saw Lewis Lake, Yellowstone Lake, Old Faithful Geyser, hot and sulfur springs, Gibbon River and Falls, Virginia Cascades, Yellowstone Grand Canyon, Yellowstone River with its upper and lower Falls, Mud Geyser, osprey, bear, elk, moose, and deer. We all took the trail which dropped 600 feet to the Lower Falls, which itself dropped another 300 feet. The rivers were raging because the snow was melting rapidly.

 The Continental Divide is the ridge of land that separates runoff water that goes to the East and the Gulf of Mexico from runoff that drains to the West and the Pacific Ocean. The continental divide meanders through Yellowstone Park such that 70% of river water drains to the Missouri River, then the Mississippi River, then to the Gulf of Mexico. This runoff going east includes all of the Yellowstone River, despite the long distance from Yellowstone to the Gulf. Most of the water going west is in the Snake River.

The park was tremendously beautiful. Yellowstone Park is centered over the Yellowstone Caldera, the largest super-volcano of the continent. The caldera is considered an active volcano. Bill and I had bad headaches because of the concentrated sightseeing looking for wildlife that eventually crossed the road right in front of us.

We didn't know it at the time, but we came within 15 miles of where Stig was staying in West Yellowstone. Stig had turned north at Yellowstone while we had turned South. When we returned to the campgrounds after 11 hours, we thanked the Nortons profusely.

The generosity shown by the Nortons and the trust they put in the bikers (three travel-worn twenty-one-year-olds) was amazing. The Nortons not only escorted us but fed us lunch with bologna sandwiches and drinks. The girls asked us to sign their autograph book, the only such honor of our journey. We ate dinner at the KOA grocery store. We then did our laundry, hoping to rid ourselves of the sulfur smell that followed us from the sulfur springs; the electricity cut off during our laundry drying.

While doing our laundry, we met a backpacker who had been treed by a bear during his hike. He was lucky to be alive because a hungry bear can easily climb a tree. Park Rangers discourage climbing a tree to escape a bear, but capsaicin bear- spray to discourage bear attacks was not available until the mid-1980s. The tent kept us dry from an overnight rainstorm. *No bicycle travel on this day, our only day off the bikes since we left Durham, NC.*

THE TRIO'S DAY 26:

June 7: No Sign of Stig

On June 7 we left camp at 10:00 AM and paid $2 each to enter the Teton National Park (we had a later refund of $1.50 each because bicycles should have cost only $0.50 each) and headed south toward Jackson Lake. The road was dirt and gravel at that time. We stopped at Signal Mountain Lodge for a snack. When we arrived at Jenny Lake, we had a panoramic view of the entire Teton Range. Jenny Lake is a large reflecting pool for the Teton Mountains which, on a calm day, results in two almost identical images of the mountains.

We went to the museum on mountaineering and saw the Nortons there by chance. We visited the park headquarters and viewed the museum. The Tetons derived their name from 19th-century French-speaking trappers for their resemblance to breasts when seen from the west side of the mountains—*les trois tetons* (the three teats). We rode to Jackson where we visited Mo's Bike Shop. Mo had not seen or heard of Stig despite being the only bicycle shop in town. Once again, an apparent hot trail turned cold and stayed that way despite Stig being close in time and place on several occasions.

Mo had a friend who had sped down the other side of Jackson Pass, which we were to climb the next day, and crashed after applying his brakes too hard.

This incident mangled his face. Vaughn tried to buy a new axle but couldn't get what he needed. Jackson is a western town with a staged shootout every day to amuse tourists, which we enjoyed. We ate dinner at the Pioneer Restaurant and then again saw the Nortons! We spent the night at St. John's Episcopal church in town. We also met three Duke students, previously unknown to us, who were seeking employment in Jackson. *Moran, WY, to Jackson, WY, 46.4 miles.*

The Norton family drove the trio through much of the Yellowstone National Park with inconvenience to themselves. The authors tried to locate them for this book with no success yet.

THE TRIO'S DAY 27:

June 8: Race to the Top

On June 8 we ate breakfast at 6:15 AM in Jackson and were climbing toward the Teton Pass by 7:00. Large stretches of the road to the pass were visible from the start of the rise and the view of the steep climb looked ominous. I felt frisky and was determined to beat Vaughn to the top of a mountain pass for the first time. Vaughn was very competitive and always wanted to be the first to the top. To reach the Pass, we climbed 2350 feet on 6 miles of roadway, with a maximum grade of 10%.

We had to stop biking and catch our breath three times but never pushed our bikes up the mountain. I led the entire way, but just before the highest point of the pass, Vaughn, predictably, moved left and started to pass Bill who was just behind me. I gave maximum effort and so did Vaughn, but Vaughn began to fall farther behind me. Both of us were puffing like steam engines when I reached the top of the pass first.

Snow was there to greet us. We passed through clouds on the way to the pass. For me, it was my most challenging climb of the journey. Bill thought the hill into Boone, NC, was the worst. Our physical conditioning was so much better for the Teton Pass climb. However, the Teton Pass seemed much more difficult to me than the Boone, NC, climb. The Pass was at 8429 feet (over a mile high, but less than Togwotee Pass) so there was less oxygen in the air compared to lower altitudes. We never let ourselves travel full speed down the other side of the mountain, using our brakes to slow down.

Vaughn's broken axle did not cause problems, but a catastrophic failure of his axle was always possible at such high speeds. We left Wyoming behind and coasted to Victor, Idaho. We then entered Swan Valley. We had a tailwind and downhill grade and made good time. We had to seek shelter to avoid the rain—it rained frequently in Idaho. We traveled adjacent to the Snake River in the afternoon, but the river soon went south of our planned route.

 The Snake River is over 1,000 miles long, originates in Yellowstone Park, is dammed 27 times creating multiple reservoirs, travels through much of Idaho, and flows into the Columbia River. Ansel Adams made a famous photograph of the river shimmering from the reflected sun with the Teton Mountains in the background.

We had lunch in Idaho Falls while trying to avoid the rain. Vaughn retrieved a letter there from the post office. Knowing that there was desolate, desert country the next day (66 miles without services), we purchased food for dinner later that day, and also breakfast for the next day. We asked the last people we saw in miles of travel where we could find shelter. The locals suggested a cave two miles ahead, but we were not satisfied with the wet cave (a mouse liked Bill's pack and food) and kept biking. There was no shelter of any kind and it kept raining. The landscape was volcanic.

Our spirits lifted when we saw a double rainbow. We knew we couldn't sleep in the rain without shelter, so we rode on well into the night. We were only able to see the middle road markings intermittently because we had no lights, and it was a very dark, overcast night creating great danger that we would run off the road. Thankfully, the road was straight. It was scary traveling a highway we were unable to see. We just hoped any oncoming vehicles had their headlights on. We finally found a rest area after the rain stopped so we sacked out at 11 PM. After four thunderstorms during the day, the rain returned during the night so we each had to use our ground cloth as a barrier to keep our sleeping bag dry. *Jackson, WY, to intersection US 26 and US 20 in Idaho, 135.4 miles.*

THE TRIO'S DAY 28:

June 9: Desolate Landscape

Golden West Cafe

BEVERAGES

SANDWICHES

Hamburger Deluxe	$1.00	Breaded Veal	$1.35
Cheeseburger Deluxe	1.10	Cubed Steak	1.35
Fishburger	1.10	Steak Sandwich	2.75
Hot Beef or Pork	1.25		

Above Sandwiches Include Salad and Potatoes

Bacon and Tomato	.85	Cheeseburger	.70
Ham and Cheese	.85	Hamburger	.60
Ham and Egg	.85	Egg Salad	.60
Fried Ham	.75	Grilled Cheese	.60
Cold Ham	.75	Tuna	.60
Cold Beef	.75	Egg	.60
Cold Pork	.75		

Side of French Fries, Jello, Cottage Cheese, Tossed Green or Potato Salad ____ .25

GOLDEN WEST DINNERS

Hamburger Steak	$1.65	Grilled Pork Chops	1.85
Roast Sirloin of Beef	1.85	Fried Chicken	1.85
Roast Leg of Pork	1.75	Prime Rib Steak	3.50
Chicken Fried Steak	1.90	Golden West T-Bone Steak	3.75
Breaded Veal Cutlets	2.00		

Soup, Salad, Vegetables, Potatoes, Roll, Coffee and Dessert Included

We Cut Our Own Steaks and Chops

FISH ORDERS

Cove Oyster Stew	$1.25	Fried Halibut	$1.75
Fried Shrimp	2.00		

Fresh Pie ____ 35c   Ala Mode ____ 45c

SALADS

Cottage Cheese and Pineapple	$1.00	Chef's Salad	1.50
Dinner Salad	.35	Shrimp Salad	2.00

FOUNTAIN SERVICE

Milk Shakes	.40	Ice Cream Sodas	.35	Ice Cream Sundae	.35
Malted Milk	.45	Root Beer Float	.35	Fountain Drinks	.10

A café menu from Arco, Idaho. Note the very low prices compared to what is expected today.

On June 9, we slept in. The landscape revealed nuclear reactor testing stations (of the Atomic Energy Commission), volcanic rock, sagebrush, and desolation. We saw perhaps 50 buses bring people from civilization to the reactor workplace. We ate the extra food from the night before as planned but had a full pancake breakfast for $0.75 at the Golden West Cafe in Arco, ID (I still have the disposable menu).

We then had a substantial headwind for the next 20 miles into Craters of the Moon National Monument. Here we learned about repeated previous volcanic activity in central Idaho. We could see two towering volcanic cones to the southeast which had served as landmarks to pioneer travelers going west. The last eruption of a local volcano was about the time Christ was on earth. Over time the volcanic activity (and tectonic plate) has moved farther west into western OR and WA.

 Craters of the Moon National Monument, named for its barren topography, is thought to resemble the moon s surface. Apollo 14 astronauts Alan Shepard and Edgar Mitchell received field training at The Craters. President Calvin Coolidge declared it a National Monument in 1924.

We were fascinated by its unique features compared to anything we had seen before.

We had to dodge another thunderstorm by hiding under a farm trailer. We knew we were vulnerable lightning rods, so we found cover. Despite this area being a desert, we surely met a lot of rain. We ate lunch in Carey and got an invitation to stay in Boise the next night with a couple (the Phillips), whom we met at the restaurant. The Phillips' nephew was attending Duke, but none of us knew him. We traveled through Picabo, not far from Sun Valley, and made it to Fairfield for dinner and the night. We slept in an abandoned house owned by the sheriff's son. The last segment of the day was enjoyable with no rain, good wind and temperature, and good road conditions. *Intersection US 26 and 20 to Fairfield, ID, 114.1 miles.*

THE TRIOS DAY 29:

June 10: Respite and Respect

On June 10, Saturday, we ate breakfast at the same cafe as the night before. We rode toward Mountain Home, which was on the way to Boise, with plans to stay with the Phillips and their parents, the Fosters. We began to climb steadily and reached an altitude of 5527 feet at Cat Creek Summit, from which we had a panoramic view. Then we began to descend into clouds (fog). Fog was dangerous for us because traffic might not see us, and we couldn't easily see obstacles such as free-range cattle, which were in the area. We had lunch at Tollgate around 11 AM.

We decided not to take a dirt road to Mayfield and instead biked Interstate 80, riding on the far-right shoulder. We sought permission from the highway patrol to bike the interstate and got tacit approval when the officer only asked us to use auxiliary roads when possible. We encountered rain, a serious headwind (20-30 mph), and very chilly temperatures. We were shivering when we stopped so decided it was best to press on. It was lucky that we didn't take the dirt (mud) road, given the rain.

The day was miserable. We traveled in close single file, using an aerodynamic posture and alternated the first rider every mile. It was ironic that we got the most rain in the state with the largest dry/desert area. Finally, eight miles east of Boise, we started downhill and the wind decreased. We exited I-80 in the city and found the Fosters' home about 8:15 PM. Once again, we were a dirty mess from a combination of sweat, mud, rain, and limited clothing.

But the Fosters welcomed us anyway. The family served plenty of chicken and shortbread. The Fosters peppered us with questions which we were happy to answer. Much of the conversation was on topics other than the bicycle trip. There was no discussion of politics despite the Vietnam War still raging, although US forces were being withdrawn; Richard Nixon was actively seeking presidential reelection; "dirty tricks" had already started, the Watergate break-in was only 7 days away (June 17); and George Wallace was recovering from an assassination attempt.

Discussing politics was taboo unless you had strong reason to believe that your views were shared. Political polarization was quite obvious and was particularly a problem between older Americans and college students who were likely to have opposite views on the Vietnam War. I took a sorely needed bath. We slept in beds for the night! The Fosters were an amazing family because they took in three dirty male strangers and treated us like royalty. *Fairfield, ID, to Boise, ID, 105.7 miles.*

CHAPTER NINE

STIG'S HOME STRETCH FROM LOLO PASS TO PORTLAND

STIG

June 9: Along the River

On June 9th I woke up in the Powell Campground in Idaho feeling unrested due to the intermittent shivering awakenings through the night. However, it was clear and a perfect day for cycling. I marveled at the sights and smells of the conifers around me and the sounds of the gushing Lochsa River. Lochsa is a Nez Perce word meaning "rough water". Lochsa is world renowned for long continuous whitewater and Lewis and Clark passed through here on their way to the Pacific in September of 1805. Here, I was about to relive some of that imagined history from the relatively comfortable seat of a bicycle and on the paved road of Highway 12 — otherwise known as the Lewis and Clark Highway. I could not wait to get started.

For the first part of the day, I cycled at a fast pace, mostly on a gradual downhill grade, on winding Highway 12 adjacent to the Lochsa River, then becoming Middle Fork Clear River near Lowell. Along the way I met a sitting cyclist on the roadside with a befuddled, exhausted look on his face next to his bicycle and backpack lying strewn on the grass. He was doing his first long distance bicycle road trip from a small town in Washington and now headed to Boise, ID. His back was sore from carrying a heavy backpack and one of his bicycle pedals had broken off. I related to his predicament (from my own beginning novice experience and backpack related pains between Durham and Greensboro), and now feeling much stronger offered to carry his backpack while he tried to pedal with one foot to the next town ahead. He accepted both offers, realizing the one pedal strategy would only be feasible if the downhill grade alongside Middle Fork Clear River continued. Except for a few stops and bike pushes along the way, we made it to Kooskia where we parted.

I continued from Kooskia to Lewiston on Highway 12 alongside the river, which had now become Clearwater River, all the way to Lewiston, ID. When I rolled into town at 6:30 PM, I felt exhausted but fulfilled from the full day of cycling. I stumbled upon the Lewis-Clark State College where I met Jim Weaver and his wife, who oversaw the Intramural Program. They offered me a place to stay in one of the dormitories as classes were not in session. The day was topped off with a homemade meal and homemade maple nut ice cream, one of my favorites. *Powell Campground, Lolo ID, to Lewiston, ID, 165 miles.*

STIG S DAY 29:

June 10: Unexpected Plans

On June 10th I woke up feeling deep gratitude for what the previous day had offered, magnificent scenery through most of the longest cycling distance yet covered, a friendly encounter with another long-distance cyclist, and a dose of hospitality from the Weavers. My memory of yesterday quickly transformed into grudging acceptance of the day before me, as it was now raining lightly with no indication of let-up, and not enough imagined hardship to keep me from launching to pedal again. While riding on Route 12 west of Clarkston, WA, the rain became more intense and I confronted a strong headwind and an uphill climb that brought back memories of the climb into Boone, NC. Nevertheless, I persevered and on the other side of the hill, during a pause from the rain, the sight of two parallel waterfalls uplifted me. However, in the course of the day, the rain resumed with periodic bouts of fog and diminished visibility, and I became very disheartened.

About 35 miles short of Pasco, WA, I stopped at a gas station for hot chocolate and cheese crackers, trying to get feeling back into my fingers. When the driver of a pickup offered me a ride to Pasco, I accepted without hesitation, forgetting for a moment any self-conceived notion of character weakness. Once in Pasco, with the cold rain continuing, I had the idea of getting a bus ride out of this weather to Grants Pass, OR. From Grants Pass, I would cycle south to see the Redwoods of Northern California and then to the Golden Gate in San Francisco, before flying back home, thereby realizing a recurring aspiration to visit San Francisco that I had while at Duke. At the Greyhound bus station, I learned that I had to meet special packaging requirements to transport my bicycle, including the dissembling of my pedals for which I had no tool. Disappointed, and feeling an uprising of guilt from breaking from the original plan, I resumed cycling toward Umatilla, OR. It was late afternoon and I had 45 miles to go.

After 10 miles of cycling, a pick-up truck with rambunctious cowboys pulled up beside me and offered a ride. They were headed to a rodeo near Umatilla and suggested I join them. I marveled at how quickly events could turn and impulsively accepted. It was a wild ride sitting in the back of their pickup as they cruised at reckless speeds on bumpy gravel roads approaching the rodeo setting. I held on to my bouncing bicycle as tightly as I could to prevent damage. Once at the rodeo I was given an honorary seat on the elevated platform from where the announcer described the events. I persevered through the evening as a gracious guest, observing the events that I did not entirely enjoy. When the rodeo was over, they let me stay on the elevated platform where I slept in my sleeping bag. During the night I woke up periodically to howling winds and a moving platform, anxious about possible rainfall since there was no canopy above me. *Lewiston-Clarkston, WA, to (via Pasco, WA) near Umatilla, OR, 103, miles cycling; 70 miles of lift.*

STIG'S DAY 30:

June 11: Help to the End

On June 11th I woke up early morning in the rodeo announcers' booth and peered over the cloth walls to take in the setting below. Nobody was around and all was quiet. It was such a contrast to the wild hoopla of the evening before. I felt alone and anxious to get moving. I relished the thought of this trip soon coming to an end and wanted to be with friends again. I quickly found my way back onto paved road and resumed my journey from Umatilla, OR, on Route 730 which became 30 toward Portland (otherwise known as the Historic Columbia River Highway). I imagined the scenery of this stretch to be spectacular due to the geology but much of this was masked by bouts of fog. Given the poor weather, I wanted to get to Portland as quickly as possible to find a flight back home to spend a few days with my mom before attending a friend's wedding in Durham, NC.

The cycling within the Columbia River Gorge toward Portland may have been the most challenging and dangerous part of the entire trip. It entailed many ups and downs, strong headwinds with periodic compromised visibility, and tunnels where lighting was difficult to adjust to with no headlight to compensate. It may have been that particular day of cycling, or traveling alone, but the conditions challenged my sanity for continuing.

More than anything, I wanted to finish the trip alive. About 80 miles short of Portland, I was offered a ride by two cyclists traveling in a car with extra bike rack space to accommodate my bicycle. With great relief, I accepted. This ride provided an additional treat as we stopped briefly at the Bonneville Fishery, near Cascade Locks, where I saw a large, live Sturgeon (7 feet and 150 pounds) for the first time in my life. We stopped again, shortly thereafter, at Multnomah Falls, the tallest in Oregon at over 600 feet.

Stig Heads Home

The cyclists dropped me off in the outskirts of Portland and I cycled downtown for about five miles to buy a plane ticket home. I came upon "The Terminal Sales Building" (a name that signaled another synchronistic event) where I was told I could buy a plane ticket. Before purchasing the ticket, I learned about the packaging needed for my bicycle. I briefly told the United Airlines salesperson about my adventure, and, in my frustration about the packaging requirements, spontaneously asked if she might be interested in buying the bicycle. I was amazed when she said yes to buying it for $100. We worked out an arrangement where she would drive home in her car, I would ride the bicycle to her place, and she would drop me off at the airport for my flight back home that night. She also agreed to mail the letter that I had carried from Butte, MT. I felt bad that I didn't deliver the letter in person as promised. I bought a plane ticket with United Airlines to West Palm Beach via Chicago for

$150. The plan worked out, including an unexpected treat of home baked chocolate chip cookies. I thought, what a miraculous way to end this trip.

That night as I flew back home, very tired, I reminisced about the entire trip, filled with wonder and gratitude for all that had happened. As we flew eastward over the Rockies, I imagined what I might do next — perhaps a world trip by bicycle, but not alone. I would need to plan the trip, find one or two other willing partners, earn the necessary money, and somehow persuade my mother that this would be a meaningful next step for my life. *Umatilla, OR, to Portland, OR 107 bicycle miles; 75 miles of lift.*

CHAPTER TEN

THE TRIO'S HOME STRETCH

BRYAN

THE TRIO'S DAY 30:

June 11: An Unexpected Plea

On June 11, we arose at 7 to a breakfast provided by the Fosters, our hosts in Boise. We left our hosts at 9:30 AM, having logged 2800 miles to that point. We resumed travel on US 26 and left the interstate and Boise behind. It was chilly as we left. We rode through beautiful farm country, following the Snake River for a time, including the towns of Caldwell, Notus, and Parma, before leaving Idaho. We entered Oregon at Nyssa and ate lunch at an A&W Restaurant. Everyone phoned home, excited about our progress. We talked to a local resident from Willamette University who was working for the forest service; we had a long conversation about the surrounding territory.

We resumed riding at 4 PM and biked through Vale, Willow Creek, and Brogan, where we ate supper at a grocery store. There were few houses and little traffic in this part of Oregon. We then rode to Ironside, encountering more mountains on the way, including Brogan Hill at 3983 feet elevation. I expected Oregon would be mountain-free but was sadly wrong.

In Ironside a grocer invited us to stay with him, which we did. He and his family were extremely interested in our bicycle trip but, when he learned that two of us would soon begin medical school, he was even more interested in discussing the health of his daughter, who had recently been diagnosed with the neurologic disorder multiple sclerosis (MS). We had a long discussion about the bike trip, politics, and MS until 11:30 PM when we went to sleep in beds once again.

The father was clearly worried about his daughter's prognosis and so were we. MS is a relapsing-remitting frequently progressive neurologic disease of unknown cause. Vaughn and I had been admitted to medical school but were clearly not experts in MS. So much is still unknown about the cause and prognosis of this illness. We were all empathetic. Bill was left with a lasting memory of the Ironsides hosts, obviously shaken by the daughter's diagnosis, virtually pleading that a cure for MS be found. *Boise, ID, to Ironside, OR, 119.1, miles.*

THE TRIO'S DAY 31:

June 12: Missing Cookies

On June 12, our host had a complimentary egg and hotcakes breakfast for us. It was very cold outside at 40 degrees when we left town, and we saw frozen water on the road. When it was so cold, it took about 20 minutes of biking exertion to fully warm us because we had no "winter" clothing.

We climbed several passes in the mountains: Eldorado (4623 feet), Blue Mountain (5098 feet), and Dixie (5277 feet). We stopped in Unity, OR, and talked to a student Forest Ranger. West of Unity, we encountered a beautiful valley and had views of the snow-covered Strawberry Mountains. There were several interesting roadside markers explaining the local geology. These were unlike markers we had seen in other states, which were usually historical markers. When we descended from mountain passes into valleys, we did not need to pedal much, and we got quite chilled.

We arrived in the town of John Day at 1 PM. Bill retrieved mail at the post office, but the expected cookies were not there. Bill arranged for the cookies to be forwarded to Astoria, OR, if they arrived. John Day was a member of the 1811 Astor Expedition that attempted to establish a worldwide trading network centered on present-day Astoria, OR. The War of 1812 doomed this project, but not before Day gained added fame by being robbed and stripped naked by Natives before being released.

We ate lunch, did our laundry, and resumed travel at 5:30 PM. We had a headwind but made good progress to Mount Vernon, where we had dinner and milkshakes. We continued on to Dayville, OR, where no one seemed interested in talking to us. We slept in a cabin two miles west of town. *Ironside, OR, to Dayville, OR, 103.9 miles.*

THE TRIO S DAY 32:

June 13: A Fine Day

We communicated to our loved ones by daily post cards and weekly Sunday phone calls. Our families knew our planned route of travel and our estimated time of arrival so they could communicate in return and send cookies and letters to us. The communications served as a detailed diary of the trip, completed by us almost always the day of travel. These were saved by Bill and me. My mother didn't lose a single postcard.

On June 13, we had a great day that began when we were awakened by a panicked bird that had somehow gotten trapped in the cabin and was bouncing off the walls. We continued to follow the John Day River past the Condon-Day Fossil beds (named John Day Fossil Beds National Park in 1975) to Kimberly, with most of the 23 miles traveled downhill. We ate breakfast at Spray. We continued to Service Creek, where a Phillips 66 truck driver gave us an accurate description of what road conditions were like ahead.

Most local people just knew about their own immediate vicinity and could not estimate how difficult the biking would be compared to driving the same routes. We ate lunch at Fossil and met the Phillips 66 man again who paid for our meals. We visited the town museum, which displayed some of the fossils that gave the town its name. Bill got a haircut to keep his hair out of the bicycle spokes. Then we rested.

We resumed riding at 4 PM and coasted into a canyon. We saw large wheat fields and giant basalt formations. We arrived in Condon about 6 PM, where a newspaper reporter took our story and pictures for two local newspapers, the *East Oregonian*, and the *Condon Globe-Times*. The papers state that we rode through 13 states and that the Teton Pass was the biggest obstacle of the trip. We told the reporter that we had only two changes of clothing. The reporter concluded:

"Anyone who has met them would agree that if our country was in the hands of young men like Simmons, Lamb and Jackson, we would have nothing to worry about. They have achieved an accomplishment which many 'soft' Americans would not even dare to dream about. It has been hard work, pedaling in all kinds of weather and sleeping with nothing but a sleeping bag between them and the hard ground, but it has been worth it."[v]

After Condon, we descended toward the John Day River and got our first view of three snow-capped mountains: Hood, Rainier (over 100 miles away), and Adams. On the way down, we entered a canyon where an intense rainstorm had caused a torrent that moved massive boulders and destroyed much of the highway in its path. We learned that a deep narrow (slot) canyon is not a safe place to be in a thunderstorm. By chance we met a professional geologist at the site of destruction caused by the torrent. He talked to us for about an hour about the dynamics of torrents entering a canyon and explained the destruction which we were observing. He blamed the road destruction on the designing engineers who placed conduits that were too small. He answered many of our questions and told us the local volcanic basalt was part of the same volcanic debris we saw in Idaho.

This was one of the finest days of the trip because of the unique experiences, cool weather, and easy biking. Never before had we seen such varied territory in a hundred-mile stretch. Days like this one produce a euphoria and a physical high which results in a feeling that any obstacle can be conquered. We spent the night at a rest area near the river. *Dayville, OR, to John Day River, OR, 114.1 miles.*

THE TRIO'S DAY 33:

June 14: Reflections as The End Nears

On June 14 we climbed six miles out of the John Day River valley and coasted to Wasco, OR, for breakfast. Several men joined us to discuss our trip and the road ahead. We rode down a steep hill to Biggs and the Columbia River and saw a red-tailed hawk. We had a stiff headwind, no doubt accentuated by the wind funneling in the river valley between large cliffs on both sides.

We crossed into Washington, the last new state on the trip, via the Samuel Hill Toll Bridge (again, no toll paid because we didn't trip the counter). We immediately had to climb a steep hill on Washington State Highway 14 and soon saw a full-sized copy of ancient Stonehenge, which was built by Samuel Hill as a monument to the locals who had served in the nation's wars. We stopped at another Hill museum, the Maryhill Museum, which we visited. Among the items at the museum were many gifts from heads of state, and chess sets from 50 countries. Sam Hill was a highly successful businessman, railroad executive, and lawyer who lived and worked in the Pacific Northwest and promoted good roads. The euphemism "What in the Sam Hill?" has nothing to do with this businessman.

We rode on, after two hours at the museum, into a strong headwind and on roads that went up and down in hilly territory. The landscape was barren with huge rocks above the highway, seemingly ready for a rockslide. We ate lunch in Washington state across the river from The Dalles, OR. We passed through several highway tunnels, the longest over 300 feet. These tunnels were anxiety-provoking because the road had only two lanes, giving drivers no easy way to safely pass us, and one was quite dark, given that we had no headlamps. By the time our eyes adjusted to the darkness, we were again in bright light.

At Bingen, WA, we started to see forests and logging operations. We ate dinner at Stevenson, WA. We saw the Bonneville Dam before stopping for the night at Beacon Rock State Park, where it cost us a total of $1.75 to stay. We had to climb three-quarters of a mile to get to the camping area on top of the huge volcanic rock, but we got to shower and sleep for the night. Giant trees were numerous, and the forest floor looked prehistoric. Railroads ran on both sides of the Columbia River and an interstate highway ran along the Oregon bank.

The Columbia River Gorge stretches over eighty miles and is up to 4,000 feet deep. The River is the only navigable route through the Cascade Mountains. In 1805, the route was used by the Lewis and Clark Expedition to reach the Pacific Ocean and on their return trip to St. Louis, MO. The Expedition camped on the Beacon Rock.

We also took advantage of the river gorge convenience to reach Portland, OR. Stig had pedaled much of the Columbia River Gorge about two days earlier, but had instead chosen a road on the south (Oregon) side of the river. We would never meet on the journey again, and not even know we all had succeeded until many years later, when I tracked Stig down through the Duke Alumni Association. *John Day River, OR, to Beacon Rock State Park, WA, 95 miles.*

The main goal of the trip was to prove that we could complete a coast-to-coast bike ride. However, we had intellectual curiosity and tried to learn as much as we could about the history, geology, and the local residents in the areas through which we traveled. We could have finished several days before we did, but we spent many, many hours talking to the "locals" at our stops. The topics of conversation were varied but almost always included information about the bike trip and our plans after the trip was completed. These topics were raised by the locals as they were naturally curious and interested in learning about our travels. We followed with questions about what we could expect if we continued our trip as planned (such as construction, detours, and challenging hills). The locals repeatedly predicted hills to be much worse than we found them. We then asked about local attractions, so we didn't miss anything of great interest. We visited many museums and landmarks. We must have crossed the Oregon trail and route of Lewis and Clark about five times each. Perhaps the most important lesson was that rural America was full of generous people who offered us a lot of support. We also learned that our fellow bikers were great and compatible companions. There wasn't a strong outward spiritual dimension to our trip, but I can say that I prayed for help from God on more than one occasion and my prayers were answered.

THE TRIO S DAY 34:

June 15: To the Coast!

On June 15, Thursday, we set a goal of reaching the Oregon coast by the end of the day. We ate breakfast at Washougal, WA, and got on an expressway into Vancouver, WA. We then rode Interstate 5 into Portland. It was the largest city that we rode through on our trip, with complicated bridges and roadways.

We rested on Hayden Island while Vaughn arranged to meet family friends the next day. We biked on a local superhighway that had a speed limit of 70 mph but exited after Vaughn almost got hit by a car which entered the exit ramp just feet in front of him. We then traveled US 26, the same road that we first traveled in Nebraska. We ate lunch in Manning, OR, had a banana split, took naps, and resumed riding at 4 PM. We had several long hills to climb, rising to 1635 feet after being close to sea-level in Portland.

We had not expected such high hills (the Coastal Range mountains) so close to the coast. We were still climbing 20 miles from the coast. Tall trees surrounded us. We encountered level land at Necandium Junction, where it became cold. We froze in the cold wind going downhill until we spotted the coast and rode into Cannon Beach. We immediately ran down to the ocean putting our hands and feet into the cold water, completing our coast-to-coast adventure at about 8 PM.

| A 50 year old pamphlet of Cannon Beach.

The coast was quite rocky at Cannon Beach and enormously beautiful. We had a seafood dinner, called home, and then headed for Ecola State Park, just north of town. We had to negotiate an extremely steep and winding road, through thick woods full of ferns, to get to the park. Bill and I walked the road to the park as we savored what we had accomplished. We slept in a picnic pavilion; the park did not allow camping, so we stretched one more rule for the trip. We had a spectacular view of the ocean from Lookout Point, even as it became dark. Reaching the coast was bittersweet. It was the ultimate high point of the trip but meant that the greatest adventure of our lives was over. *Beacon Rock Park, WA, to Cannon Beach, OR, 129.6 miles.*

THE TRIO'S DAY 35:

June 16: Sea Lions and Seagulls

On June 16, Friday, we had breakfast at Cannon Beach around 10:30, with me enjoying blueberry pancakes. We did some leisurely sightseeing and ate lunch in the town of Seaside. We saw sea lions and seagulls, just as we had imagined. Vaughn finally was able to replace his broken axle. We purchased some saltwater taffy and banana splits. We then contemplated the great mystery about why the wind always seemed to be in our faces when riding fast, even when there were no prevailing winds.

When we discovered that the last bus from Astoria to Portland left at 3:30 PM, we sprinted on our bikes to Astoria, only to discover the last bus really left at 5:30 PM. Astoria is in the same area as the historic 1805 temporary settlement of Lewis and Clark. The explorers wintered there before they returned to St. Louis. A museum in Astoria recounts their journey. We picked up mail, including Bill's cookies, which had acquired some ants. We dismantled and boxed our bicycles for the bus and airplane rides, with the help of a bike shop.

The bus followed the same route, in reverse, that we had taken the day before, but the travel seemed so much easier. We arrived at the bus depot in Portland at 8:30 PM and took a large cab (we had 3 bicycles) to the Vanns, who were Vaughn's friends and were our hosts for the night. The Vanns were out for a late evening and not home but had left us plenty of ham and cookies to eat. Bill and I put our sleeping bags on the floor and went to sleep while Vaughn waited up to talk to his family friends. *Ecola State Park, OR, to Portland, OR, 28.8 miles.*

THE TRIO'S DAY 36:

June 17: Headed Home

We got up early Saturday, had breakfast, said thanks and goodbyes to the Vanns, and took a cab to the airport. The Vanns gave us cookies and brownies for our trips home. Vaughn got a flight and left first for North Carolina. Bill was a standby passenger to Denver, his destination for the summer. I took a flight to Albany, New York, via Chicago and Cleveland. On the Cleveland flight, a lady wanted to exit the row and visit the bathroom, but I was in her way. She asked me to get up to let her pass by saying, ironically, "I hate to make you move but we all need the exercise, don't we?" I smiled but had no rejoinder.

CHAPTER ELEVEN
ROAD WARRIORS: SUMMARY REFLECTIONS

BRYAN AND STIG

The Trip in Retrospective

The trio and Stig never met after we became separated in Belleville, IL. We came very close to each other in Crete NE, Togwotee Pass, and the Columbia River Gorge, yet fate would have us miss each other. We were each unaware that we were both successful in completing the journey. Looking at this retrospectively, we remain baffled that it took so long for follow up communication. If our journey had taken place today in the era of cell phones, we would have easily reconnected and finished our journey together. When the bicycle journey was complete, the trio resumed their detailed life-plans. Immediately, they got overwhelmed with family matters, looking for work, and/or preparing for Medical school. Stig was forgotten by the trio for many years, but like a burr under the saddle, Bryan kept wondering what became of Stig, until Bryan finally used the Duke Alumni Association to track him down over ten years later. Stig got consumed with biking adventures in other continents.

The trio traveled a total of 3395 miles on the trip, not counting the 200 miles from Duke to Myrtle Beach which were counted as practice. We averaged over 100 miles for each day of biking. I, Bryan, completed the practice trips from Duke and the cross-country trip with my original equipment, except for a few new spokes, and without any flats. My entire expenses for the trip to Oregon, including food, were $240.00 (about $1500 in today's dollar). The flight home to Albany, New York, reserved the same day as travel, was an additional $173.00, including the bicycle. Shortly after the trip Bill transcribed his detailed daily diary into a neatly typed summary of our journey, which was given to all except Stig (whose fate remained unknown) and was used for many of the details in this book.

Hal was in better physical conditioning than I was and would likely have finished the entire trip if he had continued to Hannibal, after which the temperature dropped 10-15 degrees on most days.

All told, he completed 1,000 miles of the journey and then several long bicycle trips with his son later in life. I will always remember him as my college "roomie" who changed my life by talking me into becoming a pre-med student.

Stig's Trip in Retrospective

I, Stig, cycled a total of 2856 miles between Durham NC and Portland OR over a period of 27 days (105 mile per day average). My total mileage was less than that of the trio as I did not start from the East Coast nor end on the West Coast. I also received lifts totaling 360 miles, which I was especially grateful for when confronted with very inclement weather. I also kept a log that captured the highlights of each day and this was used to support my sections of this book. While I did not keep a consistent log of daily expenses, I am confident that my total expenses were less than $150 (about $900 in today's dollar) for food and a few bicycle parts and repairs, and none for any sleeping accommodations. My flight home from Portland, OR, via Chicago to West Palm Beach cost essentially the same as the entire bicycle trip.

I was not able to share the pain of serious problems (e.g., thick fog and driving rain with lightning) and the tremendous euphoria of success through companionship of co-traveling cyclists. Competitions, including the struggle to be first to the Teton Pass, and the joking camaraderie that might come with that, were not possible for me. Rather, I had to rely on my own internal goals and how I related to meeting these, or not, through my own determination to find satisfaction. Traveling alone, I felt less inclined to visit and enjoy the many museums as the trio did. On the other hand, I had more personal interactions and conversations with individuals that I met along the way. I was free of delays caused by the many problems of companion riders, such as flat tires, broken axles and calls of nature, that were experienced by the trio. On the other hand, I had to face strong headwinds alone and solve every problem myself without the advice of knowledgeable companions. I had to depend on my own determination.

Further Reflections

Getting this book into writing after all these years was another major accomplishment for Bryan and Stig, and Stig now has plans to write a book about his extensive biking outside the US. While researching the details of this book, we tried to locate some of the memorable and gracious individuals and families who gave shelter and meals, but with no success. We hope that some of you who helped us along the way will find your way to this book and then to us.

The trio thought that their cross-country bike trip was the greatest physical accomplishment of our lives. For Stig, the US trip was certainly among his most challenging physical accomplishments in all his travels. Almost everyone who completes such a bike trip today does it in separate segments and/or has an escort vehicle. Of course, one of the greatest difficulties is finding a month of free time and, preferably, at least one companion. It is also very important to select companions that you trust and can work with to solve unexpected problems. We were always able to resolve disagreements and divergent opinions. We knew each other from four years at Duke and trusted each other, which made the trip remarkably conflict-free. Any cross-country bike trip, whether done all at once or in segments, is a remarkable accomplishment. We learned that with great preparation and planning, we could accomplish what seemed to others at the time an overwhelming goal. In the process, we all discovered the generosity of the American people, the beauty of rural America, and our own determination and inner strength.

Many individuals are capable of setting a goal for a difficult physical journey to complement their academic endeavors. Books and movies are full of heroic stories of long-distance swims, bicycling, sail boating, and hikes; mountaineering; gymnastics; marathons and mountain running; expeditions; and so on. As we think about this now, all these years later, it seems to us that people considering such feats should plan to complete such a trip while they are still young and have the stamina and time. Much planning, time, practice, and possibly a companion will be needed when planning for such a vigorous physical journey. However, the memories and rewards can be gratifying, and these experiences may act as stimuli for others to plan such feats of endurance. I asked Stig who he thought was most responsible for the success of our odyssey and he said "Nobody", and "Nobody" (Odysseus) was certainly part of our inspiration. Odysseus took an epic journey of self-discovery as told by Homer in The Odyssey. This epic has inspired travelers like us over the ages.

EPILOGUE

WHAT HAPPENED TO THE FIVE BICYCLISTS

BILL

Bill left Portland at the completion of the bike trip and flew to Denver to stay with his aunt, uncle, and cousins and seek employment with the Martin-Marietta Corporation. He fell in love with the city of Denver, but the job did not pan out. Up until that time, he had spent his entire life in Chardon, OH, except the four academic years at Duke University. After the summer in Denver, Bill returned to Chardon, where after several years he completed law school. He spent his entire career commuting to Cleveland to work at the National Association of Securities Dealers (NASD) until retirement. He married and has two children. Bill did a long-distance bicycle trip with a friend, including 500 miles throughout Ohio, around 1975. He frequently rode his bike 20 miles before leaving for work at 7 AM. He helped his son earn his bicycling merit badge in Boy Scouting.

BRYAN

Bryan completed medical school at Vanderbilt University, did his residency training at Pennsylvania State University at Hershey Medical Center in Pennsylvania, worked three years at the Centers for Disease Control (CDC) in Atlanta and completed his Infectious Diseases fellowship at Emory University. He is now retired and living in Memphis, Tennessee. He is married and has two children. In 1973 he bicycled about 1,000 miles in Europe covering parts of Italy, Austria, Germany, and all of Switzerland from Zurich to Geneva.

In the US, biking provided him with a reliable way to exercise and see the areas around where he was living. He rode his bike regularly in medical school, riding 20 miles round trip to and through Percy Warner Park in Nashville, where a monster hill challenged him. He biked in the rural areas nearby while living in Hershey, PA. He biked five miles to work each way at the CDC for three years. And in Memphis he biked with the Major Taylor Bicycle Club for 2 years, named for an African American biker who is one of the greatest bicyclists of all time. Of note, in 2016, Bryan also walked with his wife 500 miles in 37 days on the Camino de Santiago in Spain.

When Bryan bicycled through Jackson Hole Wyoming and the Teton National Park in 1972, he was overwhelmed with its beauty and access to hiking, biking, kayaking, rafting and many other outdoor activities. He now owns a home there and is training to climb the Teton Pass by bicycle once again. Doing it solo will guarantee that he finishes first despite what nearly 50 years has done to his body.

Our book includes several direct and indirect references to the Odyssey by Homer. For those interested, here are the references I placed purposefully.

1. Use of Odyssey is included in the book subtitle.

2. I drank from 12 bottles of wine at my graduation ceremony as I was about to embark on my journey. Odysseus received 12 jars of wine for his journey.

3. The Greek God King of the Winds put all the winds except the Westerly into an ox skin bag to assist Odysseus on his journey home

4. Sheep were used for transportation, in reference to when Odysseus and his crew were transported from the cave of the blind cyclops by tying themselves to the belly of the sheep who carried them to temporary safety.

5. "Keep an eye out for more sheep" refers to the blinding of the cyclops by Odysseus after the cyclops was sedated with some of the 12 jars of wine mentioned above.

6. The success of our journey was partly due to "Nobody" which is the name Odysseus gave himself when asked by the cyclops for his name; use of this name caused the other cyclops to ignore calls for help from the blinded cyclops because the blinded cyclops screamed that "Nobody" was attacking him.

HAL

Hal biked in 1994 with friends from London to Wales, England, and then took a ferry to Ireland. He then biked from Cork to Dublin, Ireland. In 1997, Hal biked 430 miles from Murphy, NC, to Wilmington, NC, with his 13-year-old son Matt over nine days. Hal attended medical school at the State University of New York at Buffalo and is practicing general internal medicine in Asheville, NC.

VAUGHN

Vaughn completed medical school at Duke University, his residency training in Internal Medicine at Vanderbilt University, and his Nephrology fellowship at Baylor University. He is currently a practicing nephrologist in West Virginia.

STIG

and how this journey changed his life

Another Adventure

Stig began to plan additional long-distance biking adventures shortly after he returned home. During the first few days with his mom, Stig realized more and more the impact the trip across the US had on him. He revisited the whole trip day by day in his mind multiple times and this reinforced his idea of doing a world bicycle trip. He was not yet ready to share his idea with his mom. During his stay with his mom, he accepted a job by phone as a waiter for the Sunningdale Country Club in Scarsdale, New York. He had held this job previously during summer breaks from Duke. Since it included room and board, he could save a lot of money for the next trip. He called two of his close friends from Duke, Doug Chamberlain, and Fred Asplen, to share his US bicycle adventure and to see if they might be interested in doing a world trip together. With a bit of persistent cajoling during the summer, they both were on board and the planning began.

Another unexpected development happened soon thereafter. The woman who Stig thought he had sold his bicycle to in Portland called to say she had changed her mind. He then worked out an arrangement where Doug, who also lived in Portland at that time, picked up the bicycle to begin training for the world trip. Doug suggested that the first continent be South America since he had a close friend, Juan Borkosky, who lived in Tucuman, Argentina. Juan had lived with Doug and his family in Vienna, VA, for a year during high school through the American Field Service. Doug thought Tucuman could be a great resting point during a trip through South America. Furthermore, this might help Doug persuade his family to be more receptive to this adventure.

Ten days after working at the Sunningdale Country Club, another friend from Duke called Stig to see if he wanted to join their team to earn some quick money constructing home swimming pools in New Jersey. After a friendly negotiated departure from the Sunningdale Country Club Stig joined the team. Fred got a job shingling roofs also in New Jersey; Doug got a summer job in Portland with US Forest Service, and they all saved monies for the bicycle trip. By becoming a traveling trio, Stig, Doug, and Fred gained reluctant acceptance for their trip from their parents, similar to what Stig had done with his mom when planning the US trip.

Setting Out for South America

They launched their trip to South America on October 3rd, 1972 and cycled together in Columbia, Ecuador, and Peru. Fred left Doug and Stig in Peru to travel on his own in December. Stig and Doug continued together until Tucuman, where they stayed with the Borkosky family, recuperating, and waiting for bicycle parts shipped from the US. Doug stayed, fell in love, and eventually married before returning to the US with his spouse. Stig continued cycling on his own for two months in South America before flying back to the US on April 23rd, 1973 from Rio de Janeiro.

November 30th 1973. Stig on Pan
American Highway in desert ~ 30 KM
South of Trujillo, Peru.

December 15th, 1973. Doug, Stig, and Fred from left to right at Ticlio Pass in Peru at 15,885 feet en-route to Huancayo from Lima.

Luxembourg to Delhi

Back in the US, Stig worked to save money and launched the next leg of his bicycle trip by flying to Luxembourg on October 29th, 1973. He cycled through Europe, Turkey, Cyprus, East Africa, sailed on a freighter from Mombasa, Kenya to Mumbai (then Bombay), before ending his trip in Delhi, India on April 23rd, 1974. He then flew to Denmark to recover and be with relatives, before returning to the US.

A Career with Improbable Beginnings

Stig's world bicycle travels directly affected his career path. After having witnessed extreme poverty and poor public health conditions in the many places he traveled, he discovered the work of environmental engineering, specializing in water supply and sanitation and public health. Peace Corps volunteers, missionaries, and teachers he met during his travels, along with his mentors from the Duke Engineering faculty, inspired his pursuit of this career path. After his world bicycle travels, he returned to Duke for a Master's degree in civil engineering, with the intent to begin a career in water supply and sanitation in lesser developed countries. He received free tuition and worked during the summers and part-time during the school year to pay for his living expenses. He conducted water quality testing through the Duke Environmental Engineering Lab for clients in the area.

From January 1977 to December 1978, Stig served as a Peace Corps Volunteer, teaching Water Supply and Sanitation at the School of Engineering, Kabul University, Afghanistan, commuting by bicycle most of the days. While a Peace Corps volunteer, he traveled throughout Afghanistan, including numerous treks in the Hindu Kush. During the summer (5 weeks) and winter (8 weeks), when the University would shut down due to extreme temperatures, he traveled by public transportation throughout Pakistan, India, and Nepal, including treks in the Hindu Kush and Himalayas. After the Peace Corps stint in Afghanistan, he traveled in Asia[3] for five months (including 500 miles of trekking in the Himalayas) before returning to the US.

The New Trajectory Continues

In October 1979, Stig began working with the Office of Ground Water and Drinking Water (OGWDW) with USEPA in Washington, DC, helping to develop the US drinking water standards. During this time, he commuted by bicycle, or by running 6.5 miles each way. This got him in good enough shape to run the Boston Marathon in 2 hours and 42 minutes in 1980, despite missing the bus and needing to walk 5 miles to get to the starting area. He took a leave of absence from EPA for one year from July 1981 to July 1982 to work for Africare, building drinking water systems and implementing malaria control in the refugee camps of Somalia. After his leave of absence, he returned to EPA to work with OGWDW until June 1983, during which time he married. His wife worked for USAID and when she got a posting in Bangkok, Thailand, he accompanied her with hopes of finding consulting

---

[3]   This included Pakistan, India, Nepal, Sri Lanka, Thailand, Malaysia, Singapore, Indonesia, Australia, New Zealand, and Tahiti with intermittent assisted air travel

work. While in Thailand, he worked as a part-time consulting engineer for USAID, the Provincial Waterworks of Thailand, and a small local consulting firm. He also lived in a Buddhist monastery for six weeks practicing Insight Meditation.

Stig returned to the US and the OGWDW rehired him in February 1985 where he has continued working until his retirement in 2021. He had an amicable divorce with his first wife in 1992, mainly due to working in different countries. He married for the second time in 1997. Before getting married, they did a week bicycle trip in Denmark. Stig and his wife live in Arlington, VA, with their two teenage daughters and two dogs. For 25 years he commuted by bicycle almost every day ranging from five miles to eight miles each way, to and from EPA depending upon where he lived.

A Career in Retrospective

Stig has worked as an environmental engineer, regulation manager, and policy advisor developing US drinking water regulations. Through his work at EPA, developing drinking water regulations, participating in international conferences and workshops, Stig has realized much of his initial aspiration of contributing to the enhancement of drinking water quality in the world. He remains forever grateful for the trip across the US and the initial support he received from his friends, Bryan, Bill, Vaughn, and Hal which served as a catalyst for so much that followed.

It is not clear how the cross-country bike trip contributed to success in the careers of Bill, Bryan, Hal and Vaughn, but it clearly had a major impact on Stig's life. His commitment to long distance cycling all started by chance when a mutual friend at Duke told him about the plans of Bill, Bryan, Hal, and Vaughn for a coast-to-coast bicycle trip. Serendipity and choices can have powerful consequences, as is the theme of the Robert Frost poem *The Road Not Taken*.

APPENDIX

HOW TO PLAN A LONG-DISTANCE BICYCLE JOURNEY[VI]

We learned a lot about planning and completing long-distance biking in America and internationally. We think that our experience and advice are still valid even now. However, much of the landscape has changed. For example, food is much more expensive, sleeping in city parks is probably less tolerated, and snoozing in city jails is apparently not a common or desirable option anymore. With these changes in mind, we will share our advice about starting an adventure similar to ours.

1. First, decide how much time you have to travel, because your options and distance covered will depend on how much time you can devote to your biking adventure. If you are capable of riding 100 miles a day (a century-ride in biking lingo), you can go across the entire Unites States in about a month.

2.   You need to decide whether you are traveling with a group that provides comprehensive planning for you, usually including providing a bicycle. Bicycle adventures to Europe and other tourist areas are available and can provide everything from bicycle, lodging, bicycle repairs, some food, and a safe environment. All you need is to prepare yourself physically and pay for the trip. A travel agent should be able to locate a trip suited for you. Some charity rides can cover hundreds of miles and take care of most trip planning. Escorted biking can involve very long distances, including across America. A bicycle shop or an internet query may help you identify a trip that fits your individual needs. Use of a comprehensive bike touring company will make everything listed below unnecessary except getting physically fit.

3.   You need to buy a bicycle, tools, lock, and helmet if they are not provided for the trip you plan. Consumer Reports has an excellent discussion about selecting the best bicycle for you. Ultimately, once you become educated about the options for buying a bicycle, you will benefit greatly by talking to a knowledgeable dealer. Buying a bicycle with a lightweight frame made of carbon fiber or aluminum will cost more than a mass-market bike, but it will make climbing hills easier. Other options

worth considering are disc brakes, at least ten-speed derailleurs, a narrow and firm seat, thick and puncture-resistant tires, cycling shoes with cleats, gloves, glasses to protect your eyes, and a water bottle. If you plan to carry your own equipment (sleeping bag, tent, tools, etc.) you will need a rear bicycle rack and/or panniers. Locking your bicycle to a stationary object is recommended when not biking. If your bicycle or equipment is stolen, the entire trip can be ruined.

4. You need to get yourself physically fit for biking the planned distances. Preparation usually involves taking at least one trip covering the planned maximum daily distance. Training should probably occur over months to increase your endurance and familiarize you with your saddle (seat), changing gears, and riding on roads with traffic. A stationary bike is good for fitness training but is insufficient to practice gear changing and road practice.

5. You will need money and a budget. A credit or debit card is the preferred way to pay for food and purchases on a bike trip but carrying some cash money is a good idea. Be sure to check whether your card is valid (and whether you'll need a pin) before traveling abroad. Also, see whether cards are commonly accepted for payment if you are biking

outside the US, as even some technologically advanced countries still prefer cash. Food and lodging are almost always the two greatest expenses for a long-distance biker, even if you are part of a planned group. Sometimes a tourist group will pay some of these expenses in advance. Even eating combination meals, such as a large burger or sandwich, fries, and beverage, at McDonalds three times a day (which is not possible) costs more than $15 a day, but will not supply the estimated 5,000 calories a day that people consume on a journey covering 100 miles a day. Camping can cost $25 a night. How much you spend on food and lodging depends on your tastes. High energy snacks should be carried with you as you cycle. You will need cooking equipment if you plan to cook your own meals.

6. You will need to decide if you want companions or will travel alone. If you travel alone, you must be prepared for fighting wind resistance (drag) alone, boredom, and no one to help with falls or injuries. You should carry a cell phone in any case but pay attention to the reality that you likely will not get a signal in desolate, sparsely populated areas. The mobile phone should have GPS locating ability, as most do now. If you will have travel partners, you need to ensure that they are in good physical

condition, enough to meet your daily goals. It is also nice to have one or more companions who follow you in a van or car carrying repair and camping/sleeping equipment as needed.

7. You should have a detailed plan of travel for the entire trip, preferably using rural highways that are not heavily traveled and have a shoulder. This plan should include roads to be taken and those to be avoided (e.g., interstate highways). It is possible to just plan day-to-day or week-to-week, using local maps. In the US, you can get a detailed map from a bicycle trip planning service. You may even want to reserve a place in a motel or campground if you think you can maintain your schedule. Laundry facilities may be necessary.

8. If you plan travel outside of the United States, you will need passports and possibly visas, local currency, cellphone capability, acceptable medical insurance, return flight plans, and plans for lodging/sleeping. If you are part of a tourist biking group, these needs will be coordinated with the travel group.

9. If you plan to travel cross-country, travel from West to East to avoid the strong westerly winds, otherwise allow time for slow travel on days of strong westerly winds. You should also consider

the expected temperatures on your selected route and time of travel. You may prefer to fight westerly winds rather than very hot temperatures. The time of the year can affect snow levels on roads (even in Summer) and tree coloration.

10. Keep a detailed daily journal and take photographs and videos of memorable tourist attractions, local populations, and scenery using some method to later determine the location of the photos.

11. You will need a method of transportation to your desired location after the biking trip is finished.

Endnotes

[i]   See James Loewen's "Sundown Town" for more about this. Loewen, J. W. (2006). *Sundown Towns: A Hidden Dimension of American Racism*. Touchstone.

[ii]   Barry, J. M. (1997). *Rising tide: The great Mississippi flood of 1927* and how it changed America. Simon & Schuster.

[iii]   *Science of Cycling: Aerodynamics & Wind Resistance | Exploratorium*. (n.d.). Exploratorium: The Museum of Science, Art and Human Perception. http://www.exploratorium.edu/cycling/aerodynamics1.html

[iv]   Wilson, S. S. (1973). Bicycle technology. *Scientific American*, 228(3), 81-91.

[v]   Reprinted with permission. The Condon Globe Times is now The Times Journal

[vi]   Provided for the reader's interest only. This should not be considered a comprehensive guide.

CPSIA information can be obtained
at www.ICGtesting.com
Printed in the USA
LVHW032356020621
689203LV00001B/1